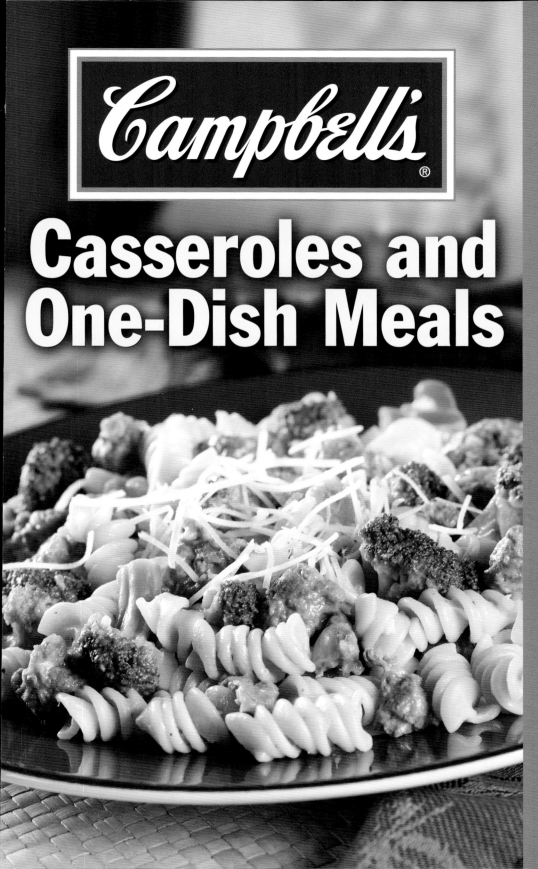

Campbell's®

Casseroles and One-Dish Meals

Contents

17

22

38

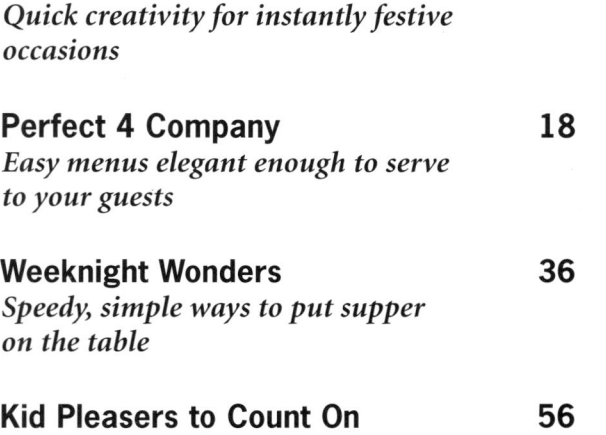

*Note: In recipes with
5 ingredients, the extra
ingredient is water.*

There's more time to enjoy family and friends
when you simplify food preparation

Less Is More

Life today runs at a pretty fast pace for all of us, and you're not alone if it seems like you have more to do and less time to do it. One of the places we really feel the crunch is in the kitchen. It's always a challenge to create well-balanced meals while balancing busy schedules, too.

When food preparation time is short, you need recipes that are long on simplicity: familiar techniques, easy steps, few ingredients and a lot less fuss. Campbell's® has come to the rescue with this collection of fast and tasty dishes made with just four ingredients or fewer. These recipes couldn't be quicker or more simple—and you probably already have many of the ingredients on hand right now in your pantry!

Best of all, this collection includes delicious and delightfully easy ideas for almost any occasion, whether you're preparing for a party, trying to feed a gang of hungry kids or just putting out a simple weeknight supper. Every recipe is designed to help you spend less time in the kitchen and more time doing what you really enjoy: connecting with your family and friends.

Chocolate and Coconut Cream Fondue
Recipe on page 8

Quick creativity for instantly festive occasions

Party Starters

It takes only three ingredients to create a party: a place to gather, the pleasure of good company and food that's festive and fun. But if you add just one more ingredient, you can make your event more than just a great get-together—you can make it an occasion that everyone will remember and enjoy, including the cook! That magic ingredient is simplicity.

This collection features entertaining favorites that never fail to get the party started—appetizers, finger foods, fun-to-share fondues, delicious dips and celebration beverages—all made with just four ingredients or fewer so pre-party preparation is quick and simple.

Napoleons California Style

Makes: 16 appetizers
Thaw: 40 minutes
Bake: 15 minutes
Prep: 10 minutes

½ of a 17.3 ounce package Pepperidge Farm® Frozen Puff Pastry
    Sheets (1 sheet)

½ cup prepared pesto sauce

½ cup drained, chopped oil-packed sun-dried tomatoes

1. Thaw the pastry sheet at room temperature for 40 minutes or until it's easy to handle. Heat the oven to 400°F. Lightly grease a baking sheet.

2. Unfold the pastry on a lightly floured surface. Cut into 3 strips along fold marks. Cut each strip into 4 rectangles. Cut each rectangle diagonally to form triangles. Put the triangles, 1 inch apart on the prepared baking sheet.

3. Bake for 15 minutes or until golden. Remove the pastry from the baking sheet and cool on a wire rack.

4. Split the pastries into 2 layers, making 48 layers in all. Set aside **16** pastry top layers. Spread pesto evenly among **16** bottom pastry layers. Top with another pastry layer and tomatoes. Top with reserved pastry top layers.

Italiano Fondue

Makes: 2 cups
Prep: 5 minutes
Cook: 10 minutes
Stand: 5 minutes

1¾ cups Prego® Traditional Italian Sauce

¼ cup dry red wine

1 cup shredded mozzarella cheese (4 ounces)

Suggested Dippers: Warm Pepperidge Farm® Garlic Bread, sliced, meatballs, sliced cooked Italian pork sausage, breaded mozzarella sticks **and/or** whole mushrooms

1. Heat the Italian sauce and wine in a 1-quart saucepan over medium heat to a boil, stirring often. Cook for 5 minutes or until the alcohol has evaporated.

2. Pour the sauce into a fondue pot or slow cooker. Stir in the cheese. Let stand for 5 minutes for cheese to melt slightly.

3. Serve warm with the *Suggested Dippers*.

Chocolate and Coconut Cream Fondue

Makes: 3 cups
Prep: 5 minutes
Cook: 10 minutes

1 can (15 ounces) cream of coconut

2 tablespoons rum (optional) **or** 1 teaspoon rum extract

1 package (12 ounces) semi-sweet chocolate pieces

Suggested Dippers: Assorted Pepperidge Farm® Cookies, Pepperidge Farm® Graham Giant Goldfish® Baked Snack Crackers, whole strawberries, banana chunks, dried pineapple pieces **and/or** fresh pineapple chunks

1. Stir the cream of coconut, rum and chocolate in a 2-quart saucepan. Heat over medium heat until the chocolate melts, stirring occasionally.

2. Pour the chocolate mixture into a fondue pot or slow cooker.

3. Serve warm with the *Suggested Dippers*.

Leftover Tip: Any remaining fondue can be used as an ice cream or dessert topping. Cover and refrigerate in an airtight container. Reheat in saucepan until warm.

Quick Cheesy Fondue

Makes: 2½ cups
Prep: 5 minutes
Cook: 10 minutes

1 can (10½ ounces) Campbell's® Condensed French Onion Soup

¼ cup dry sherry

1 package (8 ounces) cream cheese, softened

1 cup shredded Gruyère cheese (4 ounces)

Suggested Dippers: French bread cubes, warm Pepperidge Farm® Garlic Bread, cut into cubes, cooked meatballs, cubes of deli roast beef, steamed baby red potatoes

1. Heat the soup and sherry in a 2-quart saucepan over medium heat for 5 minutes or until the alcohol has evaporated. Add the cream cheese. Heat through, stirring occasionally. Add the Gruyère cheese. Cook until the cheeses melt.

2. Pour the mixture into a fondue pot or slow cooker. Serve warm with the *Suggested Dippers.*

Time-Saving Tip: To soften cream cheese, remove from wrapper. On microwavable plate, microwave on HIGH for 15 seconds.

Warm French Onion Dip
with Crusty Bread

Makes: 2 cups
Prep: 5 minutes
Bake: 30 minutes

1 can (10½ ounces) Campbell's® Condensed French Onion Soup

1 package (8 ounces) cream cheese, softened

1 cup shredded mozzarella cheese (4 ounces)

Suggested Dippers: Bread cubes, Pepperidge Farm® Crackers **or** vegetables

1. Stir the soup and cream cheese in medium bowl until smooth. Stir in the mozzarella cheese. Spread in a 1-quart shallow baking dish.

2. Bake at 375°F. for 30 minutes or until hot.

3. Serve warm with the bread, crackers or vegetables for dipping.

Time-Saving Tip: To soften the cream cheese, remove it from the wrapper and place on a microwavable plate. Microwave on HIGH for 15 seconds.

Fiesta Cilantro Fondue

Makes: 2 cups
Prep: 5 minutes
Cook: 10 minutes

1 can (10¾ ounces) Campbell's® Condensed Cream of Chicken Soup (Regular **or** 98% Fat Free)

¼ cup beer

½ cup cilantro **or** regular chunky salsa

2 cups shredded Cheddar cheese (8 ounces)

Suggested Dippers: Assorted Pepperidge Farm® Crackers, French bread cubes, cooked breaded chicken nuggets, steamed vegetables (asparagus spears, broccoli flowerets, red potato wedges) **and/or** tortilla chips

1. Stir the soup and beer in a 1-quart saucepan. Heat to a boil over medium heat. Stir in the salsa and the cheese. Heat through until the cheese melts, stirring occasionally.

2. Pour the sauce into a fondue pot or slow cooker.

3. Serve warm with *Suggested Dippers*.

Colossal Queso Dip

Colossal Queso Dip

Makes: 1½ cups
Prep: 5 minutes
Microwave: 2½ minutes

1 can (10¾ ounces) Campbell's® Condensed Cheddar Cheese Soup

½ cup chunky salsa

1 box (11.5 ounces) Pepperidge Farm® Giant Goldfish® Crackers

1. Put the soup and salsa in a 1-quart microwavable casserole. Microwave on HIGH for 2½ minutes or until hot, stirring once.

2. Serve warm with crackers for dipping.

Bloody Mary Mocktail

Makes: 3 cups
Prep: 5 minutes

3 cups V8® 100% Vegetable Juice

1 teaspoon prepared horseradish

1 teaspoon Worcestershire sauce

½ teaspoon hot pepper sauce

Ice cubes

Stir the vegetable juice, horseradish, Worcestershire and hot pepper sauce in a 4-cup measure or bowl. Pour over ice-filled tall glasses.

Pesto Elephant Ears

Makes: 24 appetizers
Thaw: 40 minutes
Prep: 20 minutes
Bake: 12 minutes

1 package (17.3 ounces) Pepperidge Farm® Frozen Puff Pastry Sheets (2 sheets)

1 egg

1 tablespoon water

3 tablespoons prepared pesto sauce

1. Thaw the pastry sheets at room temperature for 40 minutes or until they're easy to handle. Heat the oven to 400°F. Lightly grease 2 baking sheets. Stir the egg and water in a small bowl.

2. Unfold **1** pastry sheet on a lightly floured surface. Spread **half** of the pesto evenly on the pastry. Starting at the short sides, fold pastry toward center, leaving ¼-inch space in the center. Fold one side over the other, making a 4-layer rectangle. Repeat with the remaining pastry sheet and pesto.

3. Cut each rectangle into 12 (¾-inch) slices. Place slices, cut-side down, 2 inches apart on the prepared baking sheets. Brush with the egg mixture.

4. Bake for 12 minutes or until golden. Serve warm.

Campbell's Kitchen Tip: To reheat the pastries, heat the oven to 400°F. Place the pastries on a baking sheet. Bake for 2 minutes or until hot.

Sausage Bites

Makes: 36 appetizers
Thaw: 40 minutes
Prep: 20 minutes
Bake: 15 minutes

½ of a 17.3 ounce package Pepperidge Farm® Frozen Puff Pastry Sheets (1 sheet)

½ pound bulk pork sausage

1. Thaw the pastry sheet at room temperature for 40 minutes or until it's easy to handle. Heat the oven to 400°F.

2. Unfold the pastry on a lightly floured surface. Roll into a 12×9-inch rectangle. Cut into 3 (3-inch) strips.

3. Divide the sausage into thirds. Roll each into a cylinder the length of the pastry. Place on the edge of the pastry strip. Starting at the long side, roll up. Press the edges to seal.

4. Cut each roll into 12 (1-inch) slices. Place slices, cut-side down, 1½ inches apart, on 2 baking sheets. Bake for 15 minutes or until golden and sausage is cooked through. Serve warm.

Easy Substitution Tip: Substitute sweet or hot Italian pork sausage (casing removed) for the bulk pork sausage.

Make Ahead Tip: Cut into slices and place on baking sheet. Freeze. When frozen, store in plastic bag for up to 1 month. To bake, preheat oven to 400°F. Place frozen slices on baking sheets. Bake for 20 minutes or until golden and sausage is done.

Frosted Citrus Green Tea

Makes: 6 servings
Prep: 2 hours
Freeze/Refrigerate: 1 hour 30 minutes

2 bottles (16 fluid ounces **each**) Diet V8 Splash® Tropical Blend Juice Drink (4 cups), chilled

4 cups strong brewed green tea*

Fresh mint sprigs (optional)

Lemon wedges (optional)

1. Pour **2 cups** juice into 1 ice cube tray. Freeze for 1 hour 30 minutes or until the mixture is frozen.

2. Mix the remaining juice and tea in an 8-cup measure. Refrigerate for at least 1 hour and 30 minutes.

3. Unmold the cubes from the tray and place 3 to 4 cubes in each of 6 tall glasses. Divide the tea mixture among the glasses. Serve with mint and lemon, if desired.

*Strong brewed tea: Heat 4 cups of water in a 2-quart saucepan over high heat to a boil. Remove the pan from the heat. Add **8** tea bags and let them steep for 5 minutes. Remove the tea bags.*

4 Ingredients or Less 15

Zesty Chicken Mozzarella Sandwiches

Makes: 4 sandwiches
Prep: 10 minutes
Marinate: 10 minutes
Bake: 25 minutes

⅓ cup prepared Italian salad dressing

4 skinless, boneless chicken breast halves

1 loaf (11.75 ounces) Pepperidge Farm® Frozen Mozzarella Garlic Bread

1 medium red onion, sliced (about ½ cup)

1. Pour the dressing in a shallow nonmetallic dish. Add the chicken and turn to coat. Cover and refrigerate for 10 minutes.

2. Heat the oven to 400°F. While the oven is heating, lightly oil the grill rack and heat the grill to medium-hot.

3. Remove the bread from the bag. Place the frozen bread halves, cut-side up, on an ungreased baking sheet. (If the bread halves are frozen together, carefully insert fork between halves to separate.) Bake for 10 minutes or until it's hot.

4. Remove the chicken from the marinade and grill for 15 minutes or until the chicken is cooked through, turning halfway through cooking and brushing often with dressing. Discard any remaining dressing.

5. Place the chicken and red onion on the bottom bread half. Top with the remaining bread half. Cut into quarters.

Orange Mist

Makes: 10 servings
Prep: 5 minutes

1 can (46 fluid ounces) V8® 100% Vegetable Juice

1 can (6 ounces) frozen orange juice concentrate

1½ cups plain **or** orange-flavored seltzer water

Ice cubes

Orange Mist

1. Stir the vegetable juice and orange juice in a large pitcher until the mixture is smooth.

2. Add the seltzer water.

3. Pour over ice-filled tall glasses.

Honey Mustard Chicken Bites

Makes: About 40 appetizers
Prep: 15 minutes
Bake: 15 minutes

1½ pounds skinless, boneless chicken breasts, cut into 1-inch pieces

1 jar (12 ounces) refrigerated honey mustard salad dressing

2 cups Pepperidge Farm® Herb Seasoned Stuffing, crushed

2 tablespoons orange juice

1. Dip the chicken into ¾ **cup** of the dressing, then coat with the stuffing. Put the chicken on a baking sheet.

2. Bake at 400°F. for 15 minutes or until the chicken is cooked through.

3. Stir the remaining dressing and orange juice in a 1-quart saucepan over medium heat. Cook and stir until it's hot. Serve with the chicken for dipping.

Time-Saving Tip: To microwave dip, mix remaining dressing and orange juice in microwavable bowl. Microwave on HIGH for 1 minute or until hot.

Barbecued Pork Spareribs
Recipe on page 22

Perfect 4 Company

Just because a recipe is quick and simple doesn't mean it isn't special enough to serve company. It's not the complexity that makes a dish memorable, it's the combination of flavors. Likewise, the time it takes to prepare isn't important. What really matters is the love that was stirred in and the time spent sharing it at the table.

All the more reason to try one of these four wonderful company-class menus next time you plan a dinner party. The main dish, side dish and dessert recipes for each meal all require no more than four ingredients! Yet the sum of the parts adds up to a fabulous meal fit for any guest.

Fast Friday Night with Friends

Menu 1

Vegetable Platter

Barbecued Pork Spareribs*

Coleslaw

Cheddar & Roasted Garlic Biscuits*

Lemonade

Easy Apple Strudel*

*recipe provided

TGIF Entertaining Tips

• Buy a ready-made vegetable platter from the supermarket produce section on your way home from work. Add a bowl of dip or salad dressing, and you have an instant appetizer.

• Set the table, make the lemonade and prepare the grill before you leave in the morning. That way you'll have time to change out of your work clothes before everyone arrives.

• Go ahead and use good quality disposable partyware. There are wonderful colors and patterns available to brighten up your table. The prospect of easy clean up can really brighten your mood, too!

Cheddar & Roasted Garlic Biscuits

Makes: 24 biscuits
Prep: 10 minutes
Bake: 10 minutes

5 cups all-purpose baking **or** buttermilk biscuit mix

1 cup shredded Cheddar cheese (4 ounces)

1¾ cups Swanson® Seasoned Chicken Broth with Roasted Garlic

1. Heat the oven to 450°F.

2. Stir the baking mix, cheese and broth in a medium bowl to form soft dough. Drop by spoonfuls onto 2 ungreased baking sheets, making 24.

3. Bake for 10 minutes or until golden. Serve hot.

Make Ahead Tip: Baked biscuits can be frozen. To reheat, wrap loosely in aluminum foil. Heat in a 375°F. oven for 10 minutes or until hot.

Barbecued Pork Spareribs

Makes: 4 servings
Prep: 15 minutes
Cook: 30 minutes
Grill: 10 minutes

4 pounds pork spareribs

1 can (10¼ ounces) Campbell's® Beef Gravy

¾ cup barbecue sauce

2 tablespoons packed brown sugar

1. Cut the ribs into serving pieces. Heat the ribs in a 4-quart saucepan over high heat in water to cover until the water boils. Reduce the heat to low. Cover and cook for 30 minutes or until the meat is tender. Remove the ribs to paper towels to drain.

2. Stir the gravy, barbecue sauce and brown sugar in a large bowl. Add the ribs and toss gently to coat.

3. Lightly oil the grill rack and heat the grill to medium-hot. Grill the ribs for 10 minutes or until the ribs are cooked through, turning the ribs over frequently during cooking and brushing with the gravy mixture occasionally.

Campbell's Kitchen Tip: Sauce may also be used for basting chicken.

Easy Apple Strudel

Makes: 6 servings
Thaw: 40 minutes
Prep: 10 minutes
Bake: 35 minutes

½ of a 17.3 ounce package Pepperidge Farm® Frozen Puff Pastry
  Sheets (1 sheet)

1 egg

1 tablespoon water

1 can (21 ounces) apple pie filling

2 tablespoons raisins

  Confectioners' sugar

1. Thaw the pastry sheet at room temperature for 40 minutes or
until it's easy to handle. Heat the oven to 375°F. Lightly grease a
baking sheet. Stir the egg and water in a small bowl.

2. Unfold the pastry on a lightly floured surface. Roll into a
16×12-inch rectangle. With the short side facing you, spoon the pie
filling on the bottom half of the pastry to within 1 inch of the edges.
Sprinkle with the raisins. Starting at the short side, roll up like a jelly
roll. Place seam-side down on the prepared baking sheet. Tuck the
ends under to seal. Brush with the egg mixture. Cut several 2-inch
slits about 2 inches apart on top.

3. Bake for 35 minutes or until golden. Cool on the baking sheet on a
wire rack for 30 minutes. Dust with confectioners' sugar. Slice and
serve warm.

Family Sunday Dinner

Menu 2

Roast Beef with Gravy*

Green Beans

Easy Caesar Salad*

Garlic Mashed Potatoes*

Iced Tea

Pear Mini-Turnovers*

*recipe provided

Make Family the Centerpiece

When the generations get together to share a meal, create a centerpiece that helps them share memories, too. Place a decorative tray, mirror or cloth in the center of the table. Arrange several framed family photos—the older the better—on the tray. Add small vases of flowers, greenery and votive candles for color. During dinner, ask one of the children to point out a photo of someone they don't recognize. Let one of the elders introduce the person in the photo and share some fun family stories about this interesting relative!

Easy Caesar Salad

Makes: 4 servings
Prep: 10 minutes

1 small head romaine lettuce torn in bite-size pieces (about 5 cups)

1 cup Pepperidge Farm® Fat Free Caesar Croutons

½ cup prepared low-fat Caesar salad dressing

Grated Parmesan cheese

Toss the lettuce, croutons and dressing in a large bowl until evenly coated. Top with cheese. Serve immediately.

Garlic Mashed Potatoes

Makes: About 6 servings
Prep: 10 minutes
Cook: 20 minutes

3½ cups Swanson® Seasoned Chicken Broth with Roasted Garlic

5 large potatoes, cut into 1-inch pieces (about 7½ cups)

Generous dash ground black pepper

1. Heat the broth and potatoes in a 3-quart saucepan over medium-high heat to a boil.

2. Reduce the heat to medium. Cover and cook for 10 minutes or until the potatoes are tender. Drain, reserving the broth.

3. Mash the potatoes with **1¼ cups** broth and black pepper. Add additional broth, if needed, until desired consistency.

Roast Beef with Gravy

Makes: 8 servings
Prep: 5 minutes
Bake: 1 hour
Cook: 5 minutes
Stand: 10 minutes

3½- to 4-pound boneless beef bottom round **or** chuck pot roast

1¾ cups Swanson® Beef Broth (Regular, Lower Sodium **or** Certified Organic)

3 tablespoons all-purpose flour

1. Put the roast in a shallow roasting pan. Bake at 350°F. for about 1 hour or until the meat is fork-tender, basting frequently with some of the broth. Remove the roast from the pan to a cutting board and let it stand for 10 minutes before slicing.

2. Stir **1 tablespoon** of the drippings and flour in the roasting pan; discard remaining drippings. Gradually stir in the remaining broth. Cook and stir until the mixture boils and thickens. Thinly slice the roast and arrange on a serving platter. Pour the gravy into a gravy boat and serve with the roast.

Pear Mini-Turnovers

Makes: 24 pastries
Thaw: 40 minutes
Prep: 15 minutes
Bake: 12 minutes
Cool: 10 minutes

1 package (17.3 ounces) Pepperidge Farm® Frozen Puff Pastry
  Sheets (2 sheets)

2 small pears (about 8 ounces) peeled, cored and chopped

2 tablespoons raspberry preserves

  Confectioners' sugar

1. Thaw the pastry sheets at room temperature for 40 minutes or until they're easy to handle. Heat oven to 400°F. Lightly grease 2 baking sheets.

2. Put the pears and preserves in a small bowl. Stir lightly to coat.

3. Unfold the pastry sheets on a lightly floured surface. Roll each sheet into a 12-inch square and cut each into 12 rounds, using a 3-inch cookie cutter. Spoon **1 rounded teaspoon** pear mixture into center of each round. Brush edges of rounds with water and fold in half to form a half-moon. Press edges to seal. Place the turnovers, about 2 inches apart, on the prepared baking sheets.

4. Bake for 12 minutes or until golden. Remove from the baking sheet and cool on a wire rack for 10 minutes. Sprinkle with confectioners' sugar.

Book Club Dinner Meeting

Menu 3

Simply Delicious Meatloaf & Gravy*

Garlic Seasoned Vegetables*

Potato Kabobs with Cheese Sauce *

Coffee and Tea

No-Fuss Fruit Pie*

*recipe provided

4 Things to Do with Leftover Meatloaf

Cold Sandwiches: Slice meatloaf thinly and serve on your favorite Pepperidge Farm® bread with ketchup or barbecue sauce and pickle slices.

Square Meatballs: Cut meatloaf into cubes and add to your favorite Prego® pasta sauce before heating. Serve over hot cooked pasta.

Instant Hors d'oeuvres: Cut thin slices of meatloaf into squares and place atop your favorite Pepperidge Farm® crackers. Top with a dollop of horseradish sauce and a sprig of dill.

Quick Kabobs: Cut meatloaf into chunky cubes and alternate on wooden skewers with cubes of Cheddar cheese, grape tomatoes and pimiento-stuffed olives. Add a small bowl of spicy ketchup for dipping.

Garlic Seasoned Vegetables

Makes: 6 servings
Prep: 10 minutes
Cook: 10 minutes

1¾ cups Swanson® Seasoned Chicken Broth with Roasted Garlic

4 cups cut-up vegetables*

Heat the broth and vegetables in a 2-quart saucepan over high heat to a boil. Reduce the heat to low. Cover and cook for 5 minutes or until the vegetables are tender-crisp. Drain.

Use a combination of broccoli flowerets, cauliflower flowerets, sliced carrots and sliced celery.

Cooking for a Crowd: Recipe may be doubled.

Potato Kabobs with Cheese Sauce

Makes: 6 servings
Prep: 10 minutes
Grill/Cook: 35 minutes

6 medium baking potatoes (about 2 pounds)

2 tablespoons vegetable oil

1 can (10¾ ounces) Campbell's® Condensed Cheddar Cheese Soup

⅓ cup milk

1. Cut the potatoes in half lengthwise. Cut each half crosswise into 4 pieces.

2. Thread the potato pieces on **6** skewers. Brush with oil. Lightly oil a grill rack and heat the grill to medium-hot. Grill the kabobs for 30 minutes or until the potatoes are tender, turning once.

3. Stir the soup and milk in a 1-quart saucepan over medium-high heat. Cook and stir until hot. Serve the soup mixture over the potatoes.

Simply Delicious Meatloaf & Gravy

Makes: 6 servings
Prep: 5 minutes
Bake: 1 hour
Stand: 10 minutes
Cook: 5 minutes

1½ pounds ground beef

½ cup Italian-seasoned dry bread crumbs

1 egg, beaten

1 can (10¾ ounces) Campbell's® Condensed Golden Mushroom Soup

¼ cup water

1. Thoroughly mix the beef, bread crumbs and egg in a medium bowl. Put the mixture into a 13×9×2-inch baking pan and firmly shape into an 8×4-inch loaf.

2. Bake at 350°F. for 30 minutes. Spread ½ **can** of the soup over the top of meatloaf. Bake for 30 minutes or until meatloaf is cooked through. Remove the meatloaf from the pan to a cutting board and let it stand for 10 minutes before slicing.

3. Heat **2 tablespoons** of the drippings, remaining soup and water in a 1-quart saucepan over medium-high heat to a boil. Cook and stir until hot. Slice the meatloaf and arrange on a serving platter. Pour the soup mixture into a gravy boat and serve with the meatloaf.

No-Fuss Fruit Pie

Makes: 9 servings
Thaw: 40 minutes
Prep: 10 minutes
Bake: 30 minutes

1 package (17.3 ounces) Pepperidge Farm® Frozen Puff Pastry
   Sheets (2 sheets)

1 egg

1 tablespoon water

1 can **or** jar (21 ounces) fruit pie filling

1. Thaw the pastry sheets at room temperature for 40 minutes or until they're easy to handle. Heat the oven to 400°F. Lightly grease a baking sheet. Stir the egg and water in a small bowl.

2. Unfold the pastry sheets. Place **1** pastry sheet on the prepared baking sheet. Spread the pie filling on the pastry to within 1 inch of the edges. Brush the edges with the egg mixture. Place the remaining pastry sheet over the pie filling. Press the edges together with a fork to seal. Brush with the egg mixture. Cut several 2-inch slits in the top of the pastry.

3. Bake for 30 minutes or until golden. Cool on the baking sheet on a wire rack for at least 15 minutes. Cut into squares.

Souper Bowl Party

Menu 4

Game-Winning Drumsticks*

Tossed Salad

Quick Bean & Rice Casserole*

Bread and Rolls

Splash & Rainbow Punch*

Tomato Soup Spice Cake*

*recipe provided

Score Points by Serving Buffet-Style

Make your party a buffet, so your guests don't miss out on any of the action. Remember these buffet basics:

• Place the buffet table away from the wall, if possible, so guests can help themselves from both sides.

• Give guests a helping hand. Put plates at the beginning of the buffet and finish with napkins, flatware and drinks.

• Periodically check the food and replenish dishes as necessary. Make sure no serving utensils have been misplaced.

• For a fun, football-themed buffet, cover the table with a green plastic tablecloth divided into "yards" with white tape. Serve some foods from football helmets lined with foil. Identify what's in each dish with pennants cut from construction paper in the team colors and taped to wooden skewers. Cut napkins from inexpensive black and white striped cloth using pinking shears, roll them up and tie with twine. Add a plastic whistle to each one—if you dare!

Splash & Rainbow Punch

Makes: 6 servings
Prep: 5 minutes
Chill: 1 hour 30 minutes

3 cups Diet V8 Splash® Juice Drink, any flavor

3 cups sparkling mineral water **or** seltzer

2 pints assorted sorbets (lime, raspberry, strawberry, peach, lemon **or** mango)

1. Refrigerate the juice and water for 1 hour 30 minutes or until they're chilled.

2. Divide the fruit juice and mineral water among **6** tall glasses. Add **5** mini scoops (⅓ cup) of various flavors of sorbet to each glass. Serve immediately.

Serving Suggestion Tip: Use a melon baller for scooping the sorbet.

Quick Bean & Rice Casserole

Makes: 6 servings
Prep: 5 minutes
Cook: 25 minutes

2½ cups water

¾ cup **uncooked** regular long-grain white rice

1 pouch (1 ounce) Campbell's® Dry Onion Soup and Recipe Mix

1 can (15.75 ounces) Campbell's® Pork & Beans

¼ cup maple-flavored syrup

1. Heat the water in a 2-quart saucepan over high heat to a boil.

2. Stir in the rice and soup mix. Reduce the heat to low. Cover the saucepan and cook for 20 minutes or until rice is tender and most of the liquid is absorbed.

3. Stir in the beans and syrup. Cook and stir until hot.

Game-Winning Drumsticks

Makes: About 6 servings
Prep: 10 minutes
Marinate: 4 hours
Bake: 1 hour

15 chicken drumsticks (about 4 pounds)

1¾ cups Swanson® Chicken Broth (Regular, Natural Goodness™ **or** Certified Organic)

½ cup Dijon-style mustard

⅓ cup Italian-seasoned dry bread crumbs

1. Put the chicken in a single layer in a 15×10-inch disposable aluminum foil bakeware pan.

2. Stir the broth and mustard in a small bowl. Pour the broth mixture over the chicken and turn to coat. Sprinkle the bread crumbs over the chicken. Refrigerate for 4 hours.

3. Bake at 375°F. for 1 hour or until the chicken is cooked through. Serve immediately or let stand 30 minutes to serve at room temperature, using the pan juices as a dipping sauce.

Tomato Soup Spice Cake

Makes: 12 servings
Prep: 10 minutes
Bake: 25 minutes
Cool: 1 hour

1 box (about 18 ounces) spice cake mix

1 can (10¾ ounces) Campbell's® Condensed Tomato Soup (Regular **or** Healthy Request®)

½ cup water

2 eggs

Cream cheese frosting

1. Heat the oven to 350°F. Grease and lightly flour two 8- or 9-inch round cake pans.

2. Beat the cake mix, soup, water and eggs following the package directions. Spoon the batter evenly between the prepared pans.

3. Bake for 25 minutes or until a toothpick inserted in the center comes out clean.

4. Cool in pans on wire racks for 10 minutes. Remove the cakes from the pans and cool them completely on the wire racks.

5. Fill and frost the cake with your favorite cream cheese frosting.

2-Step Chicken 'n' Biscuits
Recipe on page 46

Speedy, simple ways to put supper on the table

Weeknight Wonders

Some people are really organized—and then there's the rest of us! Monday through Friday at 5 p.m., most busy folks are not only wondering where the time went, but also "what's for dinner?"

This collection of simple recipes can answer that question in no time flat! Each quick meal idea combines classic, family-pleasing flavors with true, time-saving convenience: no more than four ingredients, easy techniques and super-speedy preparation from start to finish. Now, even the most disorganized among us can get a home-cooked meal on the table every hectic, harried and hurried night of the week!

Tasty 2-Step Chicken

Makes: 4 servings
Prep: 5 minutes
Cook: 20 minutes

1 tablespoon vegetable oil

4 skinless, boneless chicken breast halves

1 can (10¾ ounces) Campbell's® Condensed Cream of
   Mushroom Soup (Regular **or** 98% Fat Free)

½ cup water

1. Heat the oil in a 10-inch skillet over medium-high heat. Add the chicken and cook for 10 minutes or until it's well browned on both sides. Remove the chicken and set aside.

2. Stir the soup and water into the skillet. Heat to a boil. Return the chicken to the skillet and reduce the heat to low. Cover and cook for 5 minutes or until the chicken is cooked through.

Sirloin Steak Picante

Makes: 6 servings
Prep: 5 minutes
Grill: 22 minutes
Stand: 10 minutes

1½ pounds boneless beef sirloin **or** top round steak, 1½ inches thick

1 jar (16 ounces) Pace® Picante Sauce **or** Chunky Salsa

1. Lightly oil the grill rack and heat the grill to medium. Grill the steak for 22 minutes for medium-rare or to desired doneness, turning the steak over halfway through cooking and brushing often with **1 cup** of the picante sauce.

2. Remove the steak from the grill to a cutting board and let it stand for 10 minutes before slicing.

3. Serve additional picante sauce with the steak.

Campbell's Kitchen Tip: To broil, heat the broiler. Place the steak on a rack in a broiler pan. Broil the steak with the top of the meat 4 inches from the heat for 25 minutes for medium or to desired doneness, turning the steak over halfway through cooking and brushing it often with the picante sauce while it's cooking.

French Onion Burgers

Makes: 4 burgers
Prep: 5 minutes
Cook: 20 minutes

1 pound ground beef

1 can (10½ ounces) Campbell's® Condensed French Onion Soup

4 slices cheese

4 round hard rolls, split

1. Shape the beef into 4 (½-inch thick) burgers.

2. Heat a 10-inch skillet over medium-high heat. Add the burgers and cook until they're well browned on both sides. Remove the burgers and set aside. Pour off any fat.

3. Stir the soup into the skillet. Heat to a boil. Return the burgers to the skillet and reduce the heat to low. Cover and cook for 5 minutes or until the burgers are cooked through. Top with cheese and continue cooking until the cheese melts. Serve burgers in rolls with soup mixture for dipping.

Enchiladas

Makes: 10 to 12 enchiladas
Prep: 15 minutes
Bake: 20 minutes

  1 pound ground beef

  1 jar (17.5 ounces) Pace® Enchilada Sauce

  2 cups shredded cheese (8 ounces)

10 to 12 corn **or** flour tortillas (6-inch), warmed

1. Heat the oven to 350°F.

2. Cook the beef in a 10-inch skillet over medium-high heat until the beef is well browned, stirring frequently to break up meat. Pour off any fat. Stir in ½ **cup** of the sauce and **1 cup** of the cheese.

3. Spread ½ **cup** of the sauce in a 13×9×2-inch (3-quart) shallow baking dish. Spoon **about 2 tablespoons** of the beef mixture down the center of each tortilla. Roll up and place seam-side down in baking dish. Top with the remaining sauce and cheese.

4. Bake for 20 minutes or until the cheese melts.

Pasta Primavera

Makes: 4 servings
Prep: 5 minutes
Cook: 20 minutes

3 cups **uncooked** corkscrew-shaped pasta (rotini)

1 bag (16 ounces) frozen vegetable combination (broccoli, cauliflower, carrots)

1 jar (1 pound 10 ounces) Prego® Traditional Italian Sauce

Grated Parmesan cheese

1. Prepare the pasta according to the package directions. Add the vegetables during the last 5 minutes of the cooking time. Drain the pasta and vegetables well in a colander.

2. Heat the sauce in the same saucepot over medium heat to a boil. Stir in the pasta and vegetables. Toss to coat. Top with the cheese.

Tomato Chicken & Noodles

Makes: 4 servings
Prep: 15 minutes
Cook: 20 minutes

Vegetable cooking spray

3 cups cut-up vegetables*

1 pound skinless, boneless chicken breasts, cut into strips

1 can (10¾ ounces) Campbell's® Condensed Tomato Soup (Regular **or** Healthy Request®)

4¼ cups water

2 packages (3 ounces **each**) chicken-flavor ramen noodle soup

1. Spray a 10-inch skillet with cooking spray and heat over medium heat for 1 minute. Add the vegetables and cook until the vegetables are tender-crisp. Set vegetables aside.

2. Remove the pan from the heat. Spray with cooking spray. Increase the heat to medium-high. Add the chicken and cook until it's well browned, stirring often. Set chicken aside.

3. Stir the tomato soup, ¼ **cup** water and **1** of the ramen seasoning packets into the skillet. (Reserve the remaining seasoning packet for another use.) Heat to a boil. Return the vegetables and chicken to the skillet. Cook and stir until the chicken is cooked through.

4. Heat **4 cups** water in a 2-quart saucepan over high heat to a boil. Add the noodles and stir.

5. Reduce the heat to medium and cook the noodles for 3 minutes or until noodles are tender but still firm, stirring occasionally. Drain the noodles well in a colander. Serve the chicken mixture over the noodles.

*Use a combination of broccoli flowerets, sliced carrots and green **or** red pepper strips.*

2-Step Nacho Pasta

Makes: 4 servings
Prep: 15 minutes
Cook: 5 minutes

1 can (11 ounces) Campbell's® Condensed Fiesta Nacho
   Cheese Soup

½ cup milk

4 cups corkscrew-shaped pasta (rotini), cooked and drained

1. Heat the soup and milk in a 2-quart saucepan over medium heat.
Cook and stir until hot and bubbling.

2. Stir in the pasta. Cook and stir until hot.

2-Step Chicken 'n' Biscuits

Makes: 4 servings
Prep: 5 minutes
Cook: 20 minutes

1 pound skinless, boneless chicken breasts, cut into cubes

1 can (10¾ ounces) Campbell's® Condensed Cream of Chicken Soup (Regular **or** 98% Fat Free)

1 bag (16 ounces) frozen vegetable combination (broccoli, cauliflower, carrots)

8 hot biscuits, split

1. Cook the chicken in a 10-inch skillet over medium-high heat until it's well browned, stirring often.

2. Stir the soup and vegetables into the skillet. Heat to a boil. Reduce the heat to low. Cover and cook for 5 minutes or until the chicken is cooked through.

3. Divide the chicken mixture among the biscuits.

2-Step Mushroom-Garlic Chicken

Makes: 4 servings
Prep: 5 minutes
Cook: 20 minutes

1 tablespoon vegetable oil

4 skinless, boneless chicken breast halves

1 can (10¾ ounces) Campbell's® Condensed Cream of Mushroom with Roasted Garlic Soup

½ cup milk

1. Heat the oil in a 10-inch skillet over medium-high heat. Add the chicken and cook for 10 minutes or until it's well browned on both sides. Remove the chicken from the skillet and set aside.

2. Stir the soup and milk into the skillet. Heat to a boil. Return the chicken to the skillet and reduce the heat to low. Cover and cook for 5 minutes or until the chicken is cooked through.

Serving Suggestion Tip: Simmer fresh broccoli in Swanson® Chicken Broth for a delicious addition to your meal. For dessert, go à la mode— scoop vanilla ice cream over piping hot Pepperidge Farm® Peach Turnovers!

Tasty 2-Step Pork Chops

Makes: 4 servings
Prep: 5 minutes
Cook: 20 minutes

1 tablespoon vegetable oil

4 bone-in pork chops, ½ inch thick

1 can (10¾ ounces) Campbell's® Condensed Cream of
   Mushroom Soup (Regular **or** 98% Fat Free)

½ cup water

1. Heat the oil in a 10-inch skillet over medium-high heat. Add the
pork chops and cook until the pork chops are well browned on both
sides. Remove the pork chops and set aside.

2. Stir the soup and water into the skillet. Heat to a boil. Return the
pork chops to the skillet and reduce the heat to low. Cover and cook
for 5 minutes or until the chops are cooked through.

Serving Suggestion Tip: Serve with vegetable combination and mashed
potatoes. For dessert, serve chocolate pudding.

2-Step Herbed Chicken

Makes: 4 servings
Prep: 5 minutes
Cook: 20 minutes

1 tablespoon vegetable oil

4 skinless, boneless chicken breast halves

1 can (10¾ ounces) Campbell's® Condensed Cream of Chicken with Herbs Soup

½ cup milk

1. Heat the oil in a 10-inch skillet over medium-high heat. Add the chicken and cook for 10 minutes or until it's well browned on both sides. Remove the chicken and set aside.

2. Stir the soup and milk into the skillet. Heat to a boil. Return the chicken to the skillet and reduce the heat to low. Cover and cook for 5 minutes or until the chicken is cooked through.

Serving Suggestion Tip: Pair this dish with a colorful side of steamed snow peas and carrots. Have a Pepperidge Farm® Milano® milkshake for dessert: Make a vanilla or chocolate milkshake and stir in crumbled Milano® cookies.

Grilled Beef Steak with Sautéed Onions

Makes: 8 servings
Prep: 5 minutes
Cook: 25 minutes

2 tablespoons olive oil

2 large onions, thinly sliced (about 2 cups)

2 pounds boneless beef sirloin, strip **or** rib steaks, cut into 8 pieces

1 jar (16 ounces) Pace® Chunky Salsa

1. Heat **1 tablespoon** of the oil in a 12-inch skillet over medium heat. Add the onions and cook until they're tender. Remove the onions from the skillet and keep warm.

2. Heat the remaining oil in the skillet. Add the steak pieces and cook until they're well browned on both sides.

3. Add the salsa and return the onions to the skillet. Cook for 3 minutes for medium-rare or until desired doneness.

Souper Sloppy Joes

Makes: 6 sandwiches
Prep: 5 minutes
Cook: 15 minutes

1 pound ground beef

1 can (10¾ ounces) Campbell's® Condensed Tomato Soup
   (Regular **or** Healthy Request®)

¼ cup water

1 tablespoon prepared yellow mustard

6 hamburger rolls, split

1. Cook the beef in a 10-inch skillet over medium-high heat until the beef is well browned, stirring frequently to break up meat. Pour off any fat.

2. Stir the soup, water and mustard into the skillet. Cook and stir until the mixture is hot and bubbling.

3. Divide the beef mixture among the rolls.

Mushroom-Garlic Pork Chops

Makes: 4 servings
Prep: 5 minutes
Cook: 20 minutes

1 tablespoon vegetable oil

4 bone-in pork chops, ½ inch thick

1 can (10¾ ounces) Campbell's® Condensed Cream of
    Mushroom with Roasted Garlic Soup

½ cup milk

1. Heat the oil in a 10-inch skillet over medium-high heat. Add the pork chops and cook until the chops are well browned on both sides. Remove the pork chops and set aside.

2. Stir the soup and milk into the skillet. Heat to a boil. Return the pork chops to the skillet and reduce the heat to low. Cover and cook for 5 minutes or until the chops are cooked through.

2-Step Cheesy Pasta Twists

Makes: 4 servings
Prep: 20 minutes
Cook: 20 minutes

4 cups corkscrew-shaped pasta (rotini), cooked and drained

1 jar (1 pound 10 ounces) Prego® Traditional Italian Sauce

1 cup shredded mozzarella cheese (4 ounces)

½ cup Pepperidge Farm® Zesty Italian Croutons, crushed

1. Heat the pasta and Italian sauce in a 10-inch skillet over medium heat until hot, stirring often.

2. Top with cheese and croutons. Reduce the heat to low. Cover and cook until the cheese melts.

2-Step Italian Burger Melt

Makes: 6 servings
Prep: 5 minutes
Bake: 20 minutes

6 ground beef patties

1 can (10¾ ounces) Campbell's® Condensed Tomato Soup (Regular **or** Healthy Request®)

⅓ cup water

1 teaspoon dried oregano leaves, crushed

1 cup shredded mozzarella cheese (4 ounces)

1. Place the patties in an 11×8-inch (2-quart) shallow baking dish. Stir the soup, water and oregano in a small bowl. Pour the soup mixture over the patties. Top with the cheese.

2. Bake at 400°F. for 20 minutes or until the patties are cooked through.

Skillet Chicken Parmesan

Makes: 6 servings
Prep: 5 minutes
Cook: 25 minutes
Stand: 5 minutes

  6 tablespoons grated Parmesan cheese

1½ cups Prego® Traditional Italian Sauce **or** Prego® Organic
     Tomato & Basil Italian Sauce

     Vegetable cooking spray

  6 skinless, boneless chicken breast halves

1½ cups shredded part-skim mozzarella cheese (6 ounces)

1. Stir **4 tablespoons** of the Parmesan cheese into the Italian sauce.

2. Spray a 12-inch skillet with cooking spray and heat over medium-high heat for 1 minute. Add the chicken and cook for 10 minutes or until well browned on both sides.

3. Pour the sauce mixture over the chicken, turning to coat with sauce. Reduce the heat to medium. Cover and cook for 5 minutes or until the chicken is cooked through.

4. Top with the mozzarella cheese and remaining Parmesan cheese. Let stand for 5 minutes or until the cheese melts.

Picante Chicken Quesadillas
Recipe on page 66

Kid
Pleasers

Fun foods that are
as simple as 1–2–3–4

to
Count On

Cooking for kids can be a challenge, but it also should be a fun and rewarding experience for everyone. Learn to make homemade foods that look good and taste great. Get your kids involved—the more they do, the better they'll eat and the prouder of their accomplishments they become. This chapter shares many easy-to-prepare simple recipes that apply the "4 ingredients or fewer" rule while incorporating tried-and-true kid favorites. Join your kids while together you whip up some tempting meals, satisfying snacks, easy treats and a surprise or two.

Goldfish® Haystacks

Makes: 24 servings
Prep: 10 minutes
Microwave: 1 minute
Stand: 1 hour

1 package (10 ounces) peanut butter chips

1 tablespoon vegetable shortening

1 cup chow mein noodles

1 package (6.6 ounces) Pepperidge Farm® Goldfish® Colors
   Baked Snack Crackers

1. Line a baking sheet with waxed paper.

2. Place the chips and shortening in a medium microwavable bowl. Microwave on HIGH for 1 minute. Stir until the chocolate is melted and smooth. Microwave an additional 15 seconds if needed.

3. Add the noodles and **1 cup** of the crackers and stir to coat.

4. Drop the mixture by **1 tablespoon** onto the prepared baking sheet. Top **each** with an additional cracker. Let stand at room temperature for 1 hour or until the mixture is set. (Or cover and refrigerate the cracker snacks until they're firm.) Store in a tightly covered container.

Easy Substitution Tip: Use your favorite flavor chips for the peanut butter chips **or** use ¾ cup Pepperidge Farm® Goldfish® Colors and ¼ cup flaked coconut.

Cheese Fries

Makes: 6 servings
Prep: 10 minutes
Bake: 20 minutes

1 bag (32 ounces) frozen French fried potatoes
1 can (10¾ ounces) Campbell's® Condensed Cheddar Cheese Soup

1. Bake the potatoes according to the package directions.

2. Push the potatoes into the center of the baking sheet. Stir the soup in the can and spoon over the potatoes.

3. Bake for 3 minutes or until the soup is hot.

Easy Substitution Tip: Substitute Campbell's® Fiesta Nacho Cheese Soup for the Cheddar Cheese Soup.

Crunchy Ranch Chicken Nuggets

Makes: 40 appetizers
Prep: 5 minutes
Bake: 15 minutes

1½ pounds skinless, boneless chicken breasts, cut into cubes

1 jar (12 ounces) refrigerated ranch salad dressing

2 cups Pepperidge Farm® Herb Seasoned Stuffing, crushed

1. Dip the chicken into ¾ **cup** of the dressing, then coat with the stuffing. Put the chicken on a baking sheet.

2. Bake at 400°F. for 15 minutes or until the chicken is cooked through.

3. Serve with the remaining dressing for dipping.

Serving Suggestion Tip: Dip grape tomatoes, celery sticks and zucchini in ranch salad dressing for a crunchy, delicious side.

5-Minute Burrito Wraps

Makes: 6 burritos
Prep: 5 minutes
Microwave: 2 minutes

1 can (11¼ ounces) Campbell's® Condensed Fiesta Chili Beef Soup

6 flour tortillas (8-inch)

Shredded Cheddar cheese

1. Spoon **2 tablespoons** of the soup down the center of each tortilla. Top with cheese. Fold the sides of the tortilla over the filling and then fold up ends to enclose the filling.

2. Put the burritos seam-side down on a microwavable plate. Microwave on HIGH for 1½ to 2 minutes or until hot.

Serving Suggestion Tip: Serve with additional Pace® Picante Sauce and black beans.

Cheeseburger Pasta

Makes: 4 servings
Prep: 5 minutes
Cook: 20 minutes

1 pound ground beef

1 can (10¾ ounces) Campbell's® Condensed Cheddar Cheese Soup

1 can (10¾ ounces) Campbell's® Condensed Tomato Soup (Regular **or** Healthy Request®)

1½ cups water

2 cups **uncooked** medium shell-shaped pasta

1. Cook the beef in a 10-inch skillet over medium-high heat until the beef is well browned, stirring frequently to break up meat. Pour off any fat.

2. Stir the soups, water and pasta into the skillet. Heat to a boil. Reduce the heat to medium. Cook for 10 minutes or until the pasta is tender but still firm, stirring often.

Serving Suggestion Tip: Serve a hearty salad of tomatoes and fresh mozzarella cheese tossed with basil, olive oil and balsamic vinegar.

Franks Under Wraps

Makes: 20 appetizers
Thaw: 40 minutes
Prep: 15 minutes
Bake: 15 minutes

½ of a 17.3 ounce package Pepperidge Farm® Frozen Puff Pastry Sheets (1 sheet)

1 egg

1 tablespoon water

10 frankfurters (about 1 pound), cut crosswise into halves

Prepared mustard

1. Thaw the pastry sheet at room temperature for 40 minutes or until it's easy to handle. Heat the oven to 400°F. Lightly grease a baking sheet. Stir the egg and water in a small bowl.

2. Unfold the pastry on a lightly floured surface. Cut into 20 (½-inch) strips. Wrap the pastry strips around the frankfurters, pressing gently to seal. Place 2 inches apart on the prepared baking sheet. Brush with the egg mixture.

3. Bake for 15 minutes or until golden. Serve with mustard for dipping.

Sloppy Joe Pizza

Makes: 4 servings
Prep: 10 minutes
Cook: 10 minutes
Bake: 12 minutes

¾ pound ground beef

1 can (10¾ ounces) Campbell's® Condensed Tomato Soup
(Regular **or** Healthy Request®)

1 Italian bread shell (12-inch)

1½ cups shredded Cheddar cheese (6 ounces)

1. Heat the oven to 450°F.

2. Cook the beef in a 10-inch skillet over medium-high until the beef is well browned, stirring frequently to break up meat. Pour off any fat.

3. Stir the soup into the skillet. Cook and stir until hot. Spread the beef mixture over the shell to within ¼ inch of the edge. Top with the cheese.

4. Bake for 12 minutes or until the cheese melts.

Power Breakfast Sandwiches

Makes: 2 sandwiches
Prep: 5 minutes

¼ cup peanut butter

4 slices Pepperidge Farm® 100% Stoneground Whole Wheat Natural Whole Grain Bread

¼ cup raisins

1 medium banana, sliced

Spread the peanut butter on **4** bread slices. Divide the raisins and banana between **2** bread slices. Top with the remaining bread slices, peanut butter-side down. Cut in half.

Easy Substitution Tip: Substitute 1 large apple, cored and sliced, for the raisins and banana.

Picante Chicken Quesadillas

Makes: 8 quesadillas
Prep: 10 minutes
Bake: 5 minutes

1 can (10¾ ounces) Campbell's® Condensed Cheddar Cheese Soup

¼ cup picante sauce

1½ cups chopped cooked chicken

8 flour tortillas (8-inch), warmed

1. Heat the oven to 425°F.

2. Stir the soup, picante sauce and chicken in a small bowl.

3. Place the tortillas on **2** baking sheets. Top **half** of each tortilla with ¼ **cup** of the soup mixture. Spread to within ½ inch of the edge. Moisten the edges of tortilla with water. Fold over and press the edges together.

4. Bake for 5 minutes or until hot.

Picante Chicken Quesadillas

Cheddar Broccoli Bake

Makes: 6 servings
Prep: 10 minutes
Bake: 30 minutes

1 can (10¾ ounces) Campbell's® Condensed Cheddar
   Cheese Soup

½ cup milk

   Dash ground black pepper

2 packages (10 ounces **each**) frozen broccoli cuts, cooked and
   drained (4 cups)

1 can (2.8 ounces) French fried onions

1. Stir the soup, milk, black pepper, broccoli and ⅔ **cup** of the onions
in a 1½-quart casserole. **Cover.**

2. Bake at 350°F. for 25 minutes or until hot. Stir the broccoli mixture.

3. Sprinkle the remaining onions over the broccoli mixture. Bake for
5 minutes more or until the onions are golden.

Easy Potato Pancakes

Makes: 4 servings
Prep: 5 minutes
Cook: 20 minutes

1¾ cups Swanson® Chicken Broth (Regular, Natural Goodness™ **or** Certified Organic)

Generous dash ground black pepper

1½ cups instant mashed potato flakes **or** buds

1 green onion, coarsely chopped (about 2 tablespoons)

1. Heat the broth and black pepper in a 2-quart saucepan over medium-high heat to a boil. Remove from the heat. Add the potato flakes and green onion and stir until liquid is absorbed. Shape the potato mixture into 4 (4-inch) pancakes.

2. Cook the pancakes in a 10-inch skillet over medium heat until they're browned on both sides.

Serving Suggestion Tip: Layer your choice of fruit and yogurt to make a delicious parfait for dessert.

Peanut Butter Banana "Tacos"

Makes: 4 tacos
Prep: 10 minutes

4 slices Pepperidge Farm® Cinnamon Swirl **or** Cinnamon Raisin Swirl Bread

4 tablespoons crunchy peanut butter

1 medium ripe banana

1. Spread the bread with the peanut butter.

2. Cut the banana into crosswise halves. Cut each half into **2** lengthwise pieces. Place **1** banana piece on each prepared bread slice and roll up.

Easy Substitution Tip: Substitute cream cheese **or** jelly for the peanut butter.

Frosty Fruit Cooler

Makes: 2 servings
Prep: 10 minutes

1 cup V8 Splash® Orange Pineapple Juice Drink

¼ cup vanilla yogurt

½ cup cut-up strawberries **or** raspberries

½ cup ice cubes

Put the juice, yogurt, strawberries and ice in an electric blender container. Cover and blend until smooth. Serve immediately.

Transporting Tip: Place in an insulated thermos, so kids can take it with them on-the-go. Recipe may be doubled.

Frosty Fruit Cooler

Mozzarella Meatball Sandwiches

Makes: 4 sandwiches
Prep: 5 minutes
Bake: 10 minutes
Cook: 20 minutes

1 loaf (11.75 ounces) Pepperidge Farm® Frozen Mozzarella Garlic Bread

1 cup Prego® Traditional Italian Sauce **or** Prego® Organic Tomato & Basil Italian Sauce

12 (½ ounce **each**) **or** 6 (1 ounce **each**) frozen meatballs

1. Heat the oven to 400°F.

2. Remove the bread from the bag. Place the frozen bread halves, cut-side up, on an ungreased baking sheet. (If the bread halves are frozen together, carefully insert a fork between the halves to separate.)

3. Bake for 10 minutes or until it's hot.

4. Heat the sauce and meatballs in a 2-quart saucepan over medium-low heat for 20 minutes or until heated through, stirring often.

5. Place the meatballs onto bottom bread half. Top with remaining bread half. Cut into quarters.

Crispy Barbecue Chicken

Makes: 4 servings
Prep: 10 minutes
Bake: 1 hour

2 pounds chicken parts

½ cup barbecue sauce

2 cups Pepperidge Farm® Herb Seasoned Stuffing, crushed

1. Dip the chicken into the barbecue sauce, then coat with the stuffing. Put the chicken in a shallow baking pan.

2. Bake at 375°F. for 1 hour or until the chicken is cooked through.

Serving Suggestion Tip: For a savory corn muffin, use Swanson® Regular **or** Seasoned Broth instead of milk when preparing your favorite corn muffin mix. Follow package directions, substituting an equal amount of broth for milk.

Fishy Families

Makes: 1 pound
Prep: 5 minutes
Microwave: 1 minute 15 seconds
Chill: 30 minutes

1 package (12 ounces) semi-sweet chocolate pieces (2 cups)

2½ cups Pepperidge Farm® Pretzel Goldfish® Baked Snack Crackers

1 container (4 ounces) multi-colored nonpareils

1. Line a baking sheet with waxed paper and set it aside. Place the chocolate in a microwavable bowl. Microwave on HIGH for 1 minute. Stir. Microwave at 15 second intervals, stirring after each, until the chocolate melts. Stir in the crackers to coat.

2. Scoop up the cracker mixture with a tablespoon and drop onto the prepared baking sheet. Sprinkle with the nonpareils. Repeat with the remaining cracker mixture and nonpareils.

3. Refrigerate for 30 minutes or until the mixture is firm. Store in the refrigerator.

Fishy Families

Jump Start Smoothies

Makes: 4 servings
Prep: 10 minutes
Chill: 1 hour 30 minutes

1 bottle (16 fluid ounces) V8 Splash® Orange Pineapple Juice Drink (2 cups)

1 cup vanilla lowfat yogurt

2 cups frozen whole strawberries **or** raspberries

1. Refrigerate the juice for 1 hour 30 minutes or until it's chilled.

2. Put the juice, yogurt and strawberries in an electric blender container. Cover and blend until smooth. Serve immediately.

Souper Nachos

Makes: 1¾ cups
Prep: 5 minutes
Microwave: 3 minutes

1 can (10¾ ounces) Campbell's® Condensed Cheddar Cheese Soup

½ cup Pace® Picante Sauce

Tortilla chips

1. Stir the soup and picante sauce in a microwavable bowl. Microwave on HIGH for 2½ to 3 minutes or until hot, stirring once.

2. Serve with chips for dipping or pour over chips.

Splash Ice Cream Soda

Makes: 8 servings
Prep: 10 minutes
Chill: 1 hour 30 minutes

2 bottles (16 fluid ounces **each**) V8 Splash® Juice Drink, any variety (4 cups)

4 cups (32 fluid ounces) lemon-lime soda

1 container (1.75 quarts) vanilla ice cream

1. Refrigerate the juice and soda for 1 hour 30 minutes or until they're chilled.

2. Stir the juice and soda in a 3-quart pitcher. Pour among **8** tall glasses. Divide the ice cream among the glasses. Serve immediately.

Cooking for a Crowd: Recipe may be doubled.

Broth Simmered Rice
Recipe on page 85

Side Dish

Fast and flavorful recipes to round out the meal

Shortcuts

Almost any entrée seems special when it's accompanied by delicious side dishes. Monday night meatloaf becomes a "blue-plate special" beside fluffy mashed potatoes and glazed carrots. A rotisserie chicken from the market tastes like Sunday dinner when it's paired with stuffing. Easy tacos are especially good complemented with spiced up Mexican-style rice. Yet we often don't have time—or at least we think we don't have time—to make interesting and appealing side dishes part of the weekday menu.

These side dish shortcuts are not only long on flavor, they're also some of the easiest dishes to put on the table. They include wonderful ideas that can double as vegetarian entrées and some deceptively simple sides that will even impress your guests.

Creamy Vegetables in Pastry Shells

Makes: 6 servings
Prep: 10 minutes
Bake: 15 minutes
Cook: 10 minutes

1 package (10 ounces) Pepperidge Farm® Frozen Puff Pastry Shells

1 can (10¾ ounces) Campbell's® Condensed Cream of Mushroom Soup (Regular **or** 98% Fat Free)

⅓ cup milk **or** water

1 bag (16 ounces) frozen vegetable combination (broccoli, cauliflower, carrots), cooked and drained

1. Bake the pastry shells according to the package directions.

2. Heat the soup and milk in a 2-quart saucepan over medium heat. Cook and stir until hot and bubbling. Divide the vegetables among the pastry shells. Spoon the sauce over vegetables and pastry shells.

Cheesy Broccoli

Makes: 6 servings
Prep: 5 minutes
Microwave: 8 minutes

1 can (10¾ ounces) Campbell's® Condensed Cheddar
  Cheese Soup

¼ cup milk

2 packages (10 ounces **each**) frozen broccoli cuts (4 cups)

1. Stir the soup and milk in a 2-quart microwavable casserole.
Add the broccoli. Cover the dish with plastic wrap.

2. Microwave on HIGH for 8 minutes or until the broccoli is
tender-crisp, stirring once.

Souper Quick Gumbo Rice

Makes: 3 servings
Prep: 5 servings
Cook: 5 minutes
Stand: 5 minutes

1 can (10¾ ounces) Campbell's® Condensed Chicken
   Gumbo Soup

1 cup water

⅛ teaspoon garlic powder

⅛ teaspoon onion powder

1¼ cups **uncooked** instant white rice

1. Heat the soup, water, garlic powder and onion powder in a
2-quart saucepan over medium-high heat to a boil.

2. Stir in the rice. Cover the saucepan and remove from the heat.
Let stand for 5 minutes. Fluff the rice with a fork.

Broth Simmered Rice

Broth Simmered Rice

Makes: 4 servings
Prep: 5 minutes
Cook: 20 minutes

1¾ cups Swanson® Chicken Broth (Regular, Natural Goodness™ **or** Certified Organic)

¾ cup **uncooked** regular long-grain white rice

1. Heat the broth in a 2-quart saucepan over medium-high heat to a boil.

2. Stir in the rice. Reduce the heat to low. Cover the saucepan and cook for 20 minutes or until the rice is tender and most of the liquid is absorbed.

Easy Substitution Tip: Substitute Swanson® Beef, Vegetable **or** Seasoned Broths for the Chicken Broth.

Cooking for a Crowd: Double the recipe.

Fiesta Tomato Rice

Makes: 4 servings
Prep: 5 minutes
Cook: 5 minutes
Stand: 5 minutes

1 can (10½ ounces) Campbell's® Condensed Chicken Broth

½ cup water

½ cup chunky salsa

2 cups **uncooked** instant white rice

1. Heat the broth, water and salsa in a 2-quart saucepan over medium-high heat to a boil.

2. Stir in the rice. Cover the saucepan and remove from the heat. Let stand for 5 minutes. Fluff the rice with a fork.

Saucy Asparagus

Saucy Asparagus

Makes: 6 servings
Prep: 5 minutes
Cook: 10 minutes

1 can (10¾ ounces) Campbell's® Condensed Cream of Asparagus Soup

⅓ cup milk **or** water

2 pounds asparagus, trimmed **or** 2 packages (about 10 ounces **each**) frozen asparagus spears, cooked and drained

Stir the soup and milk in a 2-quart saucepan over medium heat. Cook and stir until the mixture is hot. Serve over the asparagus.

Onion Bean Bake

Makes: 11 servings
Prep: 10 minutes
Bake: 1 hour

2 cans (28 ounces **each**) Campbell's® Pork & Beans

1 pouch (1 ounce) Campbell's® Dry Onion Soup and Recipe Mix

2 tablespoons maple-flavored syrup

4 slices bacon, cut in half and partially cooked

1. Stir the beans, soup mix and syrup in an 11×8-inch (2-quart) shallow baking dish. Top with the bacon.

2. Bake at 350°F. for 1 hour or until hot.

Creamy Souper Rice

Creamy Souper Rice

Makes: 4 servings
Prep: 5 minutes
Cook: 5 minutes
Stand: 5 minutes

1 can (10¾ ounces) Campbell's® Condensed Cream of Mushroom Soup (Regular **or** 98% Fat Free)

1 soup can water

1 soup can **uncooked** instant white rice

1. Heat the soup and water in a 2-quart saucepan over medium-high heat to a boil.

2. Stir in the rice. Cover the saucepan and remove from the heat. Let stand for 15 minutes or until rice is done. Fluff the rice with a fork.

Souper Quick Southwestern Rice & Beans

Makes: 3 servings
Prep: 5 minutes
Cook: 5 minutes
Stand: 5 minutes

1 can (10¾ ounces) Campbell's® Condensed Southwestern-Style Chicken Vegetable Soup

1 cup water

1¼ cups **uncooked** instant white rice

1. Heat the soup and water in a 2-quart saucepan over medium-high heat to a boil.

2. Stir in the rice. Cover the saucepan and remove from the heat. Let stand for 5 minutes. Fluff the rice with a fork.

Savory Vegetables

Savory Vegetables

Makes: 4 servings
Prep: 5 minutes
Cook: 10 minutes

1 cup Swanson® Chicken Broth (Regular, Natural Goodness™ **or** Certified Organic)

3 cups cut-up vegetables*

1. Heat the broth and vegetables in a 2-quart saucepan over high heat to a boil.

2. Reduce the heat to low. Cover and cook for 5 minutes or until the vegetables are tender-crisp. Drain.

Use a combination of vegetables you like, including broccoli flowerets, cauliflower flowerets, sliced carrots, bell pepper strips, onion wedges and snow peas.

Fiesta Potatoes

Makes: 5 servings
Prep: 20 minutes
Cook: 10 minutes

1 can (10¾ ounces) Campbell's® Condensed Cheddar Cheese Soup

½ cup chunky salsa

¼ cup milk

5 medium potatoes, cooked and sliced ¼ inch thick

1. Heat the soup, salsa and milk in a 10-inch skillet over medium heat. Cook and stir until hot and bubbling.

2. Add the potatoes. Cook until they're hot.

Skinny Mashed Sweet Potatoes

Skinny Mashed Sweet Potatoes

Makes: 6 servings
Prep: 5 minutes
Cook: 25 minutes

3½ cups Swanson® Chicken Broth (Regular, Natural Goodness™ **or** Certified Organic)

4 large sweet potatoes or yams, cut into 1-inch pieces (about 7½ cups)

Generous dash ground black pepper

2 tablespoons packed brown sugar

1. Heat the broth and potatoes in a 3-quart saucepan over high heat to a boil. Reduce the heat to medium. Cover and cook for 10 minutes or until the potatoes are tender. Drain, reserving broth.

2. Mash the potatoes with **1¼ cups** of the broth and black pepper. Add additional broth, if needed, until desired consistency. Stir in the brown sugar.

Mushroom-Garlic Oven Baked Risotto

Makes: 4 servings
Prep: 5 minutes
Bake: 45 minutes
Stand: 5 minutes

1 can (10¾ ounces) Campbell's® Condensed Cream of Mushroom with Roasted Garlic Soup

3⅓ cups water

½ teaspoon dried thyme leaves, crushed

1¼ cups **uncooked** regular long-grain white rice

¼ cup slivered almonds

1. Stir the soup, water, thyme, rice and almonds in a 2-quart casserole. **Cover.**

2. Bake at 375°F. for 45 minutes or until the rice is tender and most of the liquid is absorbed. Stir. Let the risotto stand for 5 minutes before serving.

Fruited Chunky Salsa

Makes: 2¾ cups
Prep: 10 minutes
Stand: 15 minutes

1 jar (12 ounces) chunky salsa, any variety

2 tablespoons chopped fresh cilantro leaves

1 teaspoon lime juice

1 mango, diced (about 1 cup)

Stir the salsa, cilantro, lime juice and mango in a small bowl. Let stand for 15 minutes. Serve the salsa as a condiment for pork, poultry **or** seafood.

Garden Vegetable Stuffing

Makes: 8 servings
Prep: 10 minutes
Cook: 10 minutes
Bake: 20 minutes

    Vegetable cooking spray

1¾ cups Swanson® Chicken Broth (Regular, Natural Goodness™ **or** Certified Organic)

3 cups cut-up vegetables*

5 cups Pepperidge Farm® Cubed Herb Seasoned Stuffing

1. Spray a 1½-quart casserole with cooking spray.

2. Heat the broth and vegetables in a 3-quart saucepan over high heat to a boil. Reduce the heat to low. Cover and cook for 5 minutes or until the vegetables are tender-crisp. Remove from the heat.

3. Add the stuffing and stir lightly to coat. Spoon into the prepared casserole.

4. Bake at 350°F. for 20 minutes or until hot.

Use a combination of broccoli flowerets, sliced carrots, cauliflower flowerets and sliced celery.

Fastest Homemade Mac 'n' Cheese

Makes: 4 servings
Prep: 5 minutes
Cook: 20 minutes

1 can (10¾ ounces) Campbell's® Condensed Cheddar
    Cheese Soup

½ soup can milk

½ soup can water

1 cup **uncooked** elbow macaroni

1. Heat the soup, milk and water in a 2-quart saucepan over medium heat to a boil.

2. Add the macaroni and stir. Reduce the heat to low. Cook for 10 minutes or until the macaroni is tender but still firm, stirring often.

Campbell's®

4 Ingredients or Less

Contents

108

137

186

**Shrimp & Corn Chowder
with Sun-Dried Tomatoes**
Recipe on page 130

Fuss-free preparation and easy clean-up means…

Complete Satisfaction

Wouldn't you love to never have to compromise when making dinner? For convenience sake, we might be tempted to skimp on side dishes or sacrifice variety for simplicity. But one-dish meals are a win-win solution.

One-dish recipes streamline menu planning and food preparation, and they cut down on clean-up. Yet they still satisfy everyone's basic craving for hot, hearty, home-cooked meals. Layers of flavors and a well-rounded profile that usually includes protein, vegetable and starch all add up to total satisfaction for everyone.

This Campbell's® collection of one-dish recipes features favorite casseroles that go fresh from the oven to the table with minimal fuss, skillet suppers that whip together quickly on the stovetop, plus yummy soups, stews and chilis that only require a basket of bread or rolls to turn into dinner. You'll also discover ethnically inspired dishes from around the world and easy updates on the classics sure to win everyone over, including the cook!

Home-baked and hearty casseroles

Favorites
From the Oven

Roast Pork with Green Apples & Golden Squash

Makes: 8 servings
Prep: 20 minutes
Bake: 45 minutes
Stand: 10 minutes

Vegetable cooking spray

2 (¾ pound **each**) whole pork tenderloins

1 teaspoon olive oil

¼ teaspoon coarsely ground black pepper

3 large Granny Smith apples, cored and thickly sliced

1 butternut squash (about 1½ pounds), peeled, seeded and cut into 1-inch cubes (about 4 cups)

2 tablespoons packed brown sugar

½ teaspoon ground cinnamon

1¾ cups Swanson® Chicken Broth (Regular, Natural Goodness™ **or** Certified Organic)

2 teaspoons all-purpose flour

1. Heat the oven to 425°F. Spray a 17×11-inch roasting pan with cooking spray.

2. Brush the pork with the oil and sprinkle with the black pepper. Put the pork in the prepared pan.

3. Put the apples, squash, brown sugar, cinnamon and ½ **cup** of the broth in a large bowl. Toss to coat with the broth mixture. Add the squash mixture to the pan.

4. Bake for 25 minutes or until the pork is cooked through, stirring the squash mixture once while it's cooking. Remove the pork from the pan to a cutting board and let it stand for 10 minutes before slicing. Continue to bake the squash mixture for 15 minutes more or until browned. Remove the squash mixture from the pan with a slotted spoon.

5. Stir the flour into the drippings in the roasting pan. Cook and stir over medium heat for 1 minute then gradually stir in the remaining broth. Cook and stir until the mixture boils and thickens. Thinly slice the pork and arrange on a serving platter with the vegetables. Pour the sauce into a gravy boat and serve with the pork.

Chicken and Peppers Pie

Makes: 6 servings
Prep: 10 minutes
Bake: 30 minutes

1 can (10¾ ounces) Campbell's® Condensed Cream of Chicken Soup (Regular **or** 98% Fat Free)

½ cup picante sauce

½ cup sour cream

2 teaspoons chili powder

1 jar (7 ounces) whole roasted sweet peppers, drained and cut into strips

4 medium green onions, sliced (about ½ cup)

3 cups cubed cooked chicken

1 package (11 ounces) refrigerated cornbread twists **or** breadsticks

Fresh sage leaves (optional)

1. Stir the soup, picante sauce, sour cream, chili powder, peppers, green onions and chicken in an 11×8-inch (2-quart) shallow baking dish.

2. Bake at 400°F. for 15 minutes. Stir.

3. Separate the cornbread twists into **16** strips. Arrange the strips, lattice-fashion, over the chicken mixture, overlapping strips as necessary to fit.

4. Bake for 15 minutes more or until the cornbread is golden. Top with sage, if desired.

Baked Pork Chops with Apple Raisin Stuffing

Makes: 4 servings
Prep: 15 minutes
Bake: 35 minutes

 1 cup applesauce

½ cup water

 2 tablespoons butter, melted

 1 stalk celery, chopped (about ½ cup)

 2 tablespoons raisins

 4 cups Pepperidge Farm® Herb Seasoned Stuffing

 4 boneless pork chops, ¾ inch thick

   Paprika **or** ground cinnamon

   Apple slices (optional)

1. Stir the applesauce, water, butter, celery and raisins in a medium bowl. Add the stuffing and stir lightly to coat. Spoon the stuffing mixture into an 11×8-inch (2-quart) shallow baking dish. Arrange the pork chops over the stuffing. Sprinkle paprika over the chops.

2. Bake at 400°F. for 35 minutes or until the pork is cooked through. Top with apple slices, if desired.

Cornbread Chicken Pot Pie

Makes: 4 servings
Prep: 10 minutes
Bake: 30 minutes

1 can (10¾ ounces) Campbell's® Condensed Cream of Chicken Soup (Regular **or** 98% Fat Free)

1 can (about 8 ounces) whole kernel corn, drained

2 cups cubed cooked chicken **or** turkey

1 package (8½ ounces) corn muffin mix

¾ cup milk

1 egg

½ cup shredded Cheddar cheese

1. Heat the oven to 400°F. Stir the soup, corn and chicken in a 9-inch pie plate.

2. Stir the muffin mix, milk and egg with a fork in a small bowl until the ingredients are mixed. Spoon over the chicken mixture.

3. Bake for 30 minutes or until the cornbread is golden. Sprinkle with the cheese.

Garlic Mashed Potatoes & Beef Bake

Makes: 4 servings
Prep: 5 minutes
Cook: 10 minutes
Bake: 20 minutes

1 pound ground beef **or** ground turkey

1 can (10¾ ounces) Campbell's® Condensed Cream of Mushroom
 with Roasted Garlic Soup

1 tablespoon Worcestershire sauce

1 bag (16 ounces) frozen vegetable combination (broccoli,
 cauliflower, carrots), thawed

2 cups water

3 tablespoons butter

¾ cup milk

2 cups instant mashed potato flakes **or** buds

1. Cook the beef in a 10-inch skillet over medium-high heat until the beef is well browned, stirring frequently to break up meat. Pour off any fat.

2. Stir the beef, ½ **can** of the soup, Worcestershire and vegetables in an 11×8-inch (2-quart) shallow baking dish.

3. Heat the water, butter and remaining soup in a 2-quart saucepan over high heat to a boil. Remove from the heat. Stir in the milk. Slowly stir in the potatoes. Spoon the potatoes over the beef mixture.

4. Bake at 400°F. for 20 minutes or until hot.

Time-Saving Tip: To thaw vegetables, microwave on HIGH for 3 minutes.

Serving Suggestion Tip: Serve with a mixed green salad topped with orange sections, walnut pieces and raspberry vinaigrette. For dessert, serve your favorite fruit dish.

Tomato-Topped Chicken & Stuffing

Makes: 4 servings
Prep: 10 minutes
Bake: 30 minutes

- 5 cups Pepperidge Farm® Cubed Herb Seasoned Stuffing
- 6 tablespoons butter, melted
- 1¼ cups boiling water
- 4 skinless, boneless chicken breast halves
- 1 can (10¾ ounces) Campbell's® Condensed Cream of Chicken Soup (Regular **or** 98% Fat Free)
- ⅓ cup milk
- 1 medium tomato, sliced

1. Coarsely crush **1 cup** of the stuffing. Mix crushed stuffing with **2 tablespoons** of the butter in a small bowl. Set aside.

2. Stir the remaining butter and water in a medium bowl. Add the stuffing and stir lightly to coat.

3. Spoon the stuffing mixture into a 13×9×2-inch (3-quart) shallow baking dish. Top with the chicken.

4. Stir the soup and milk in a small bowl. Pour over the chicken. Top with the tomato. Sprinkle with the reserved stuffing mixture.

5. Bake at 400°F. for 30 minutes or until the chicken is cooked through.

3-Cheese Pasta Bake

Makes: 4 servings
Prep: 15 minutes
Bake: 20 minutes

1 can (10¾ ounces) Campbell's® Condensed Cream of Mushroom Soup (Regular **or** 98% Fat Free)

1 package (8 ounces) shredded two-cheese blend

⅓ cup grated Parmesan cheese

1 cup milk

¼ teaspoon ground black pepper

3 cups corkscrew-shaped pasta (rotini), cooked and drained

1. Stir the soup, cheeses, milk and black pepper in a 1½-quart casserole. Stir in the pasta.

2. Bake at 400°F. for 20 minutes or until hot.

Easy Substitution Tip: Use **2 cups** of your favorite shredded cheese for the 8-ounce package.

Shrimp Stuffing au Gratin

Makes: 6 servings
Prep: 15 minutes
Bake: 30 minutes

4½ cups Pepperidge Farm® Herb Seasoned Stuffing

3 tablespoons butter, melted

1¼ cups water

2 cups cooked broccoli flowerets

2 cups cooked medium shrimp

1 can (10¾ ounces) Campbell's® Condensed Cream of Mushroom Soup (Regular **or** 98% Fat Free)

½ cup milk

2 tablespoons diced pimiento (optional)

1 cup shredded Swiss cheese (4 ounces)

1. Coarsely crush ½ **cup** of the stuffing. Mix the stuffing and **1 tablespoon** of the butter in a small cup. Set aside.

2. Stir the water and remaining butter in an 11×8-inch (2-quart) shallow baking dish. Add the remaining stuffing and stir lightly to coat.

3. Arrange the broccoli and shrimp over the stuffing.

4. Stir the soup, milk, pimiento, if desired and cheese in a small bowl. Pour the soup mixture over the shrimp mixture. Sprinkle with the reserved stuffing mixture.

5. Bake at 350°F. for 30 minutes or until hot.

Campbell's Kitchen Tips: You'll need to purchase 1 pound of fresh medium shrimp to have enough for 2 cups of cooked shrimp needed for this recipe. Heat 4 cups water in a 2-quart saucepan over high heat to a boil. Add the shrimp and cook for 1 to 3 minutes or until the shrimp turn pink. Drain in a colander and rinse under cold water. Remove the shells and devein the shrimp.

For 2 cups cooked broccoli flowerets use 3 cups fresh broccoli flowerets.

To melt the butter, remove it from the wrapper and place in a microwavable cup. Cover and microwave on HIGH for 45 seconds.

Lemon-Basil Turkey with Roasted Vegetables

Makes: 8 servings
Prep: 20 minutes
Bake: 1 hour 30 minutes
Stand: 10 minutes

Vegetable cooking spray

2 medium lemons

8-pound fresh turkey breast*

24 baby Yukon Gold potatoes

1 butternut squash (about 1¼ pounds), peeled, seeded and cut into 1-inch cubes (about 3 cups)

8 medium beets, peeled and cut into 1-inch cubes (about 3¾ cups)

12 small white onions, peeled **or** 1 cup frozen small whole onions

1 tablespoon butter, melted

1 tablespoon dried basil leaves, crushed

1 cup Swanson® Chicken Broth (Regular, Natural Goodness™ **or** Certified Organic)

1. Spray a 17×11-inch roasting pan with cooking spray.

2. Cut **1** lemon into thin slices. Squeeze **2 tablespoons** juice from remaining lemon. Loosen skin on turkey breast and place lemon slices under the skin.

3. Place the turkey, meat-side up, potatoes, squash, beets and onions in the prepared pan. Brush the turkey with the butter and sprinkle with the basil. Insert a meat thermometer into the thickest part of the meat, making sure the thermometer is not touching the bone.

4. Stir the broth and lemon juice in a small bowl. Pour half of the broth mixture over the turkey and vegetables.

5. Roast the turkey at 375°F. for 1 hour. Stir the vegetables.

6. Add the remaining broth mixture to the pan. Roast for 30 minutes more or until the thermometer reaches 180°F. Let the turkey stand for 10 minutes before slicing.

*If using a frozen turkey breast, thaw before cooking.

Time-Saving Tip: To quickly peel the onions, put the onions in a medium bowl. Pour boiling water over them. Let stand for 5 minutes. Drain and then slip off the skins.

Thyme Chicken & Roasted Winter Vegetables

Makes: 4 servings
Prep: 20 minutes
Bake: 1 hour 30 minutes

Vegetable cooking spray

3-pound whole broiler-fryer chicken

1 tablespoon butter, melted

4 medium red potatoes (about 1¼ pounds), cut into quarters

4 medium carrots (about ¾ pound), peeled and cut into 2-inch pieces

6 medium parsnips (about 1 pound), peeled and cut into 2-inch pieces

1 cup Brussels sprouts, cut in half

4 medium onions, cut into quarters

1 tablespoon chopped fresh thyme leaves **or** 1 teaspoon dried thyme leaves, crushed

1 cup Swanson® Chicken Broth (Regular, Natural Goodness™ **or** Certified Organic)

½ cup Chablis **or** other dry white wine

1. Spray a 17×11-inch roasting pan with cooking spray. Remove backbone from the chicken, using poultry shears. Place the chicken flat with skin-side up in the prepared pan. Brush with the butter.

2. Place the potatoes, carrots, parsnips, Brussels sprouts and onions around the chicken. Sprinkle with the thyme. Stir the broth and wine in a 2-cup measure. Pour ¾ **cup** of the broth mixture over the chicken and vegetables.

3. Roast the chicken at 375°F. for 1 hour or until the chicken is cooked through. Remove the chicken from the pan and keep warm.

4. Stir the vegetables. Add the remaining broth mixture to the pan. Roast for 30 minutes more or until the vegetables are tender.

Baked Chicken & Cheese Risotto

Makes: 4 servings
Prep: 10 minutes
Bake: 45 minutes
Stand: 5 minutes

1 can (10¾ ounces) Campbell's® Condensed Cream of Mushroom Soup (Regular **or** 98% Fat Free)

1¼ cups water

½ cup milk

1½ cups frozen mixed vegetables

½ pound skinless, boneless chicken breasts, cut into cubes

¼ cup shredded mozzarella cheese

3 tablespoons grated Parmesan cheese

¾ cup **uncooked** Arborio **or** regular long-grain white rice

1. Stir the soup, water, milk, vegetables, chicken, cheeses and rice in a 13×9×2-inch (3-quart) shallow baking dish. **Cover.**

2. Bake at 400°F. for 35 minutes. Stir.

3. Bake for 10 minutes more or until hot and the rice is tender but still firm. Let the risotto stand for 5 minutes before serving.

Fiesta Chicken Casserole

Makes: 6 servings
Prep: 20 minutes
Bake: 40 minutes

1 package (15 ounces) refrigerated pie crusts

1 jar (16 ounces) chunky salsa

1 can (10¾ ounces) Campbell's® Condensed Cream of Chicken Soup (Regular **or** 98% Fat Free)

1 cup sour cream

2 cups shredded Cheddar cheese (8 ounces)

1 package (24 ounces) frozen whole kernel corn

2 cans (9.75 ounces **each**) Swanson® Premium Chunk Chicken Breast, drained

1 can (about 15 ounces) black beans, rinsed and drained

1. Heat the oven to 400°F. Let the pie crusts stand at room temperature for 15 minutes or until they're easy to handle.

2. Stir the salsa, soup, sour cream, cheese, corn, chicken and beans in a large bowl. Spoon the soup mixture into a 13×9×2-inch (3-quart) shallow baking dish.

3. Place the crusts on a lightly floured surface, overlapping about 3 inches in the center. Press the seam to seal. Roll into a 14×10-inch rectangle. Trim excess crust. Place the crust over the chicken mixture. Crimp or roll the edges to seal it to the dish. Cut slits in the crust with a knife.

4. Bake for 40 minutes or until the crust is golden brown.

Country Chicken Casserole

Makes: 5 servings
Prep: 10 minutes
Cook: 5 minutes
Bake: 25 minutes

1 can (10¾ ounces) Campbell's® Condensed Cream of Celery Soup (Regular **or** 98% Fat Free)

1 can (10¾ ounces) Campbell's® Condensed Cream of Potato Soup

1 cup milk

¼ teaspoon dried thyme leaves, crushed

⅛ teaspoon ground black pepper

4 cups cut-up vegetables*, cooked and drained

2 cups cubed cooked chicken **or** turkey

1½ cups water

4 tablespoons butter

4 cups Pepperidge Farm® Herb Seasoned Stuffing

1. Stir the soups, milk, thyme, black pepper, vegetables and chicken in a 13×9×2-inch (3-quart) shallow baking dish.

2. Heat the water and butter in a 2-quart saucepan over high heat to a boil. Add the stuffing and stir lightly to coat. Spoon the stuffing over the chicken mixture.

3. Bake at 400°F. for 25 minutes or until hot.

Use a combination of cut green beans and sliced carrots.

Beef Taco Bake

Makes: 4 servings
Prep: 5 minutes
Cook: 5 minutes
Bake: 30 minutes

1 pound ground beef

1 can (10¾ ounces) Campbell's® Condensed Tomato Soup (Regular **or** Healthy Request®)

1 cup Pace® Chunky Salsa **or** Picante Sauce

½ cup milk

6 (8-inch) flour tortillas **or** 8 (6-inch) corn tortillas, cut into 1-inch pieces

1 cup shredded Cheddar cheese (4 ounces)

1. Cook the beef in a 10-inch skillet over medium-high heat until the beef is well browned, stirring frequently to break up meat. Pour off any fat.

2. Stir the soup, salsa, milk, tortillas and ½ **cup** of the cheese into the skillet. Spoon the soup mixture into an 11×8-inch (2-quart) shallow baking dish. **Cover.**

3. Bake at 400°F. for 30 minutes or until hot. Sprinkle with the remaining cheese.

Chicken Asparagus Gratin

Makes: 4 servings
Prep: 20 minutes
Bake: 30 minutes

- 1 can (10¾ ounces) Campbell's® Condensed Cream of Asparagus Soup
- ½ cup milk
- ¼ teaspoon onion powder
- ⅛ teaspoon ground black pepper
- 1½ cups asparagus cuts, cooked and drained
- 1½ cups cubed cooked chicken
- 2½ cups corkscrew-shaped pasta (rotini), cooked and drained
- 1 cup shredded Cheddar **or** Swiss cheese (4 ounces)

1. Stir the soup, milk, onion powder, black pepper, asparagus, chicken, pasta and ½ **cup** of the cheese in an 11×8-inch (2-quart) shallow baking dish.

2. Bake at 400°F. for 25 minutes or until hot. Stir.

3. Sprinkle with the remaining cheese. Bake for 5 minutes more or until the cheese melts.

Turkey Stuffing Divan

Makes: 6 servings
Prep: 10 minutes
Bake: 30 minutes

4 cups Pepperidge Farm® Herb Seasoned Stuffing

1¼ cups water

4 tablespoons butter

1 package (10 ounces) frozen broccoli cuts, cooked and drained (2 cups)

2 cups cubed cooked turkey **or** chicken

1 can (10¾ ounces) Campbell's® Condensed Cream of Celery Soup (Regular **or** 98% Fat Free)

½ cup milk

1 cup shredded Cheddar cheese (4 ounces)

1. Prepare the stuffing using the water and butter according to the package directions.

2. Spoon the stuffing into an 11×8-inch (2-quart) shallow baking dish. Arrange the broccoli and turkey over the stuffing mixture.

3. Stir the soup, milk and ½ **cup** of the cheese in a small bowl. Pour over the turkey mixture. Sprinkle with the remaining cheese.

4. Bake at 350°F. for 30 minutes or until hot.

Easy Substitution Tip: Use about **1 pound** fresh broccoli, trimmed and cut into 1-inch pieces for the frozen broccoli.

Chicken Florentine Lasagna

Makes: 6 servings
Prep: 10 minutes
Bake: 1 hour
Stand: 5 minutes

2 cans (10¾ ounces **each**) Campbell's® Condensed Cream of Chicken with Herbs Soup

2 cups milk

1 egg

1 container (15 ounces) ricotta cheese

6 **uncooked** lasagna noodles

1 package (about 10 ounces) frozen chopped spinach, thawed and well drained

2 cups cubed cooked chicken **or** turkey

2 cups shredded Cheddar cheese (8 ounces)

1. Stir the soup and milk in a medium bowl.

2. Stir the egg and ricotta cheese in a small bowl.

3. Spread **1 cup** of the soup mixture in a 13×9×2-inch (3-quart) shallow baking dish. Top with **3** noodles, the ricotta mixture, spinach, chicken, **1 cup** of the Cheddar cheese and **1 cup** of the soup mixture. Top with remaining 3 noodles and remaining soup mixture. **Cover.**

4. Bake at 375°F. for 1 hour. Uncover the dish and sprinkle with the remaining Cheddar cheese. Let the lasagna stand for 5 minutes before serving.

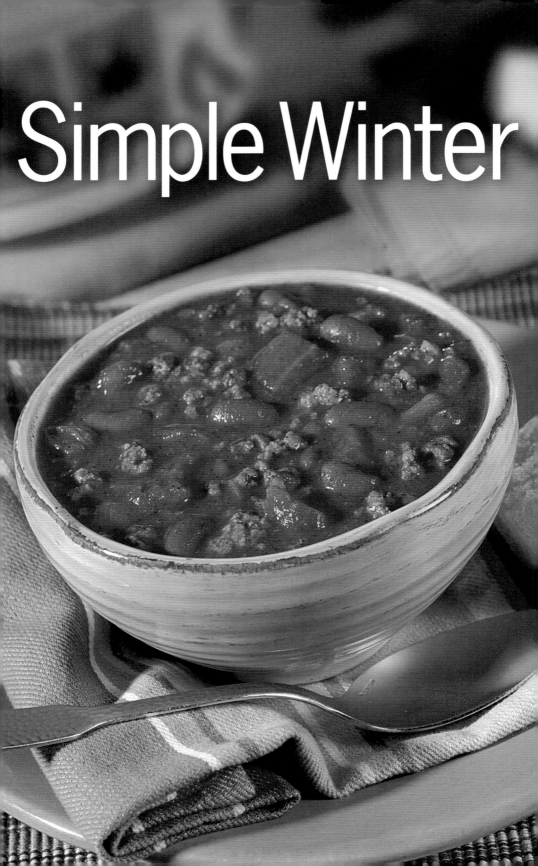

Simple Winter

Bowls of comfort to take away the chill

Stews and Soups

Slow Cooker Hearty Beef & Bean Chili

Makes: 6 servings
Prep: 15 minutes
Cook: 8 to 10 hours

1½ pounds ground beef

1 can (10¾ ounces) Campbell's® Condensed Tomato Soup (Regular **or** Healthy Request®)

½ cup water

¼ cup chili powder

2 teaspoons ground cumin

2 cloves garlic, minced

1 large onion, chopped (about 1 cup)

2 cans (about 15 ounces **each**) red kidney beans, rinsed and drained

1 can (14½ ounces) diced tomatoes

1. Cook the beef in a 10-inch skillet in 2 batches over medium-high heat until the beef is well browned, stirring frequently to break up meat. Remove the beef with a slotted spoon and put in a 3½-quart slow cooker.

2. Stir the soup, water, chili powder, cumin, garlic, onion, beans and tomatoes into the cooker.

3. Cover and cook on LOW for 8 to 10 hours*.

Or on HIGH for 4 to 5 hours

20-Minute Seafood Stew

Makes: 4 servings
Prep: 10 minutes
Cook: 15 minutes

2 cups Prego® Traditional Italian Sauce

1 bottle (8 fluid ounces) clam juice

¼ cup Burgundy **or** other dry red wine (optional)

1 pound fish **and/or** shellfish*

8 small clams in shells, well scrubbed

Chopped fresh parsley

1. Heat the Italian sauce, clam juice and wine in a 3-quart saucepan over medium-high heat to a boil. Reduce the heat to low. Cook for 5 minutes.

2. Add the fish and clams. Cover and cook for 5 minutes or until the fish flakes easily when tested with fork and clams are open. Discard any clams that do not open. Sprinkle with parsley.

*Use any one **or** a combination of the following: Firm white fish fillets (cut into 2-inch pieces), boneless fish steaks (cut into 1-inch cubes), medium shrimp (shelled and deveined) **or** scallops.*

Campbell's Kitchen Tip: Before cooking, discard any clams that remain open when tapped.

Hearty Bean & Barley Soup

Makes: 6 servings
Prep: 15 minutes
Cook: 40 minutes

1 tablespoon olive oil

2 large carrots, coarsely chopped (about 1 cup)

2 stalks celery, sliced (about 1 cup)

1 large onion, chopped (about 1 cup)

3 cloves garlic, minced

3½ cups Swanson® Vegetable Broth (Regular **or** Certified Organic)

1 can (about 15 ounces) red kidney beans, rinsed and drained

1 can (14½ ounces) diced tomatoes

¼ cup **uncooked** pearl barley

2 cups firmly packed chopped fresh spinach leaves

Ground black pepper

1. Heat the oil in a 4-quart saucepan over medium-high heat. Add the carrots, celery, onion and garlic. Cook and stir until the vegetables are tender.

2. Stir the broth, beans, tomatoes and barley into the saucepan. Heat to a boil. Reduce the heat to low. Cover and cook for 30 minutes or until the barley is done.

3. Stir in the spinach and cook until the spinach wilts. Season to taste with black pepper.

Spaghetti Soup

Makes: 4 servings
Prep: 15 minutes
Cook: 30 minutes

- 2 tablespoons vegetable oil
- ½ pound skinless, boneless chicken breasts, cut into cubes
- 1 medium onion, chopped (about ½ cup)
- 1 large carrot, chopped (about ½ cup)
- 1 stalk celery, finely chopped (about ⅓ cup)
- 2 cloves garlic, minced
- 4 cups Swanson® Chicken Broth (Regular, Natural Goodness™ **or** Certified Organic)
- 1 can (10¾ ounces) Campbell's® Condensed Tomato Soup (Regular **or** Healthy Request®)
- 1 cup water
- 3 ounces **uncooked** spaghetti, broken into 1-inch pieces
- 2 tablespoons chopped fresh parsley (optional)

1. Heat **1 tablespoon** of the oil in a 4-quart saucepan over medium-high heat. Add the chicken and cook until it's well browned, stirring often. Remove the chicken with a slotted spoon and set aside.

2. Add the remaining oil and heat over medium heat. Add the onion and cook for 1 minute. Add the carrots and cook for 1 minute. Add the celery and garlic and cook for 1 minute.

3. Stir the broth, soup and water into the saucepan. Heat to a boil. Stir in the pasta. Cook for 10 minutes or until the pasta is tender. Add the chicken and parsley, if desired, and cook until the chicken is cooked through.

Picante Pork Stew

Makes: 4 servings
Prep: 20 minutes
Cook: 25 minutes

3 tablespoons cornstarch

1¾ cups Swanson® Vegetable Broth (Regular **or** Certified Organic)

2 tablespoons vegetable oil

1 pound boneless pork loin, cut into very thin strips

4 cups cut-up fresh vegetables*

½ cup picante sauce

1. Stir the cornstarch and broth in a small bowl. Set the mixture aside.

2. Heat **1 tablespoon** of the oil in a 6-quart saucepot over medium-high heat. Add the pork and cook until it's well browned, stirring often. Remove the pork with a slotted spoon and set aside.

3. Reduce the heat to medium. Add the remaining oil. Add the vegetables and cook until tender-crisp. Pour off any fat.

4. Add the picante sauce. Stir the cornstarch mixture and stir into the saucepot. Cook and stir until the mixture boils and thickens. Return the pork to the saucepot and heat through.

*Use asparagus cut into 2-inch pieces, red pepper cut into 2-inch-long strips and sliced onions.

Shrimp & Corn Chowder with Sun-Dried Tomatoes

Makes: 4 servings
Prep: 5 minutes
Cook: 20 minutes

 1 can (10¾ ounces) Campbell's® Condensed Cream of Potato Soup

1½ cups half-and-half

 2 cups whole kernel corn

 2 tablespoons sun-dried tomatoes, cut into strips

 1 cup small **or** medium cooked shrimp

 2 tablespoons chopped fresh chives

Ground black **or** ground red pepper

1. Heat the soup, half-and-half, corn and tomatoes in a 2-quart saucepan over medium heat to a boil. Reduce the heat to low. Cover and cook for 10 minutes.

2. Stir in the shrimp and heat through.

3. Season to taste with black pepper.

Easy Substitution Tip: For a lighter version, substitute skim milk for the half-and-half.

Spicy Mexican Minestrone Stew

Makes: 6 servings
Prep: 15 minutes
Cook: 35 minutes

½ pound sweet Italian pork sausage, casing removed

2 teaspoons vegetable oil

1¾ cups Swanson® Beef Broth (Regular, Lower Sodium **or** Certified Organic)

1½ cups picante sauce

½ teaspoon garlic powder **or** 2 cloves garlic, minced

1 can (14½ ounces) whole peeled tomatoes, undrained and cut up

1 cup **uncooked** medium shell-shaped pasta

1 package (about 10 ounces) frozen cut green beans, thawed (about 2 cups)

1 can (about 15 ounces) red kidney beans, rinsed and drained

1. Shape the sausage firmly into ½-inch meatballs.

2. Heat the oil in a 6-quart saucepot over medium-high heat. Add the meatballs and cook until they're well browned. Remove the meatballs with a slotted spoon and set aside. Pour off any fat.

3. Stir the broth, picante sauce, garlic and tomatoes into the saucepot. Heat to a boil. Stir in the pasta. Return the meatballs to the saucepot and reduce the heat to low. Cover and cook for 10 minutes, stirring often.

4. Stir in the green beans and kidney beans. Cook and stir for 10 minutes more or until the pasta is tender but still firm.

Easy Substitution Tip: Substitute 1 can (about 16 ounces) cut green beans, drained, for the frozen beans.

Time-Saving Tip: Instead of shaping into meatballs, cook the sausage in the oil until it's well browned, stirring frequently to break up meat. Pour off any fat.

Italian Sausage & Lentil Stew

Makes: 8 servings
Prep: 15 minutes
Cook: 1 hour

Vegetable cooking spray

1 pound sweet Italian pork sausage, cut into 1-inch pieces

2 large carrots, sliced (about 1 cup)

1 large onion, chopped (about 1 cup)

2 cloves garlic, minced

3½ cups Swanson® Vegetable Broth (Regular **or** Certified Organic)

2 teaspoons dried oregano leaves, crushed **or** 2 tablespoons chopped fresh oregano

1 bay leaf

2 cups cubed red potatoes

½ cup dried lentils

2 cups coarsely chopped broccoli rabe

1. Spray a 6-quart saucepot with cooking spray and heat over medium-high heat for 1 minute. Add the sausage and cook until it's well browned, stirring frequently to break up meat. Pour off any fat.

2. Add the carrots, onion and garlic and cook until tender.

3. Stir the broth, oregano, bay leaf, potatoes and lentils into the saucepot. Heat to a boil. Reduce the heat to low. Cover and cook for 40 minutes or until the lentils are tender.

4. Stir in the broccoli rabe. Cook for 5 minutes more or until tender. Remove the bay leaf.

Herb-Simmered Beef Stew

Makes: 6 servings
Prep: 15 minutes
Cook: 1 hour 30 minutes

2 pounds beef for stew, cut into 1-inch pieces

Ground black pepper

2 tablespoons all-purpose flour

2 tablespoons olive oil

8 ounces mushrooms, thickly sliced (about 3 cups)

3 cloves garlic, minced

½ teaspoon **each** dried marjoram, thyme **and** rosemary leaves, crushed **or** 1½ teaspoons **each** chopped fresh marjoram, thyme **and** rosemary

1 bay leaf

1¾ cups Swanson® Beef Broth (Regular, Lower Sodium **or** Certified Organic)

3 cups fresh **or** frozen baby carrots

12 whole baby red potatoes, with a strip of peel removed in center

1. Sprinkle the beef with the black pepper. Lightly coat the beef with the flour.

2. Heat the oil in a 6-quart saucepot over medium-high heat. Add the beef in 2 batches and cook until it's well browned, stirring often. Remove the beef with a slotted spoon and set aside.

3. Add the mushrooms, garlic, marjoram, thyme, rosemary and bay leaf and cook until the mushrooms are tender and the liquid evaporates.

4. Stir the broth into the saucepot. Heat to a boil. Return the beef to the pot and reduce the heat to low. Cover and cook for 45 minutes.

5. Add the carrots and potatoes. Cover and cook for 30 minutes more or until the meat and vegetables are fork-tender. Stir the stew occasionally while cooking. Remove the bay leaf.

Country Chicken Stew

Makes: 4 servings
Prep: 15 minutes
Cook: 40 minutes

2 slices bacon, diced

1 medium onion, sliced (about ½ cup)

1 can (10¾ ounces) Campbell's® Condensed Cream of Chicken Soup (Regular **or** 98% Fat Free)

1 soup can water

½ teaspoon dried oregano leaves, crushed

3 medium potatoes (about 1 pound), cut into 1-inch pieces

2 medium carrots, sliced (about 1 cup)

1 cup frozen cut green beans

2 cans (4.5 ounces **each**) Swanson® Premium Chunk Chicken Breast, drained

2 tablespoons chopped fresh parsley

1. Cook the bacon in a 10-inch skillet over medium-high heat until it's crisp. Remove the bacon with a slotted spoon and drain on paper towels.

2. Add the onion and cook in the hot drippings until tender.

3. Stir the soup, water, oregano, potatoes and carrots into the skillet. Heat to a boil. Reduce the heat to low. Cover and cook for 15 minutes.

4. Add the beans. Cover and cook for 10 minutes or until the vegetables are tender. Add bacon, chicken and parsley. Cook until hot.

Easy Substitution Tip: Substitute 1 can (8 ounces) cut green beans, drained, for the frozen beans. Add to the skillet with the chicken.

Smokin' Texas Chili

Makes: 6 servings
Prep: 15 minutes
Cook: 1 hour 50 minutes

2 tablespoons olive oil

1½ pounds boneless beef sirloin **or** top round steak, ¾-inch thick, cut into ½-inch pieces

1 medium onion, chopped (about ½ cup)

2 cloves garlic, minced

3 cups Pace® Chunky Salsa, any variety

½ cup water

1 tablespoon chili powder

1 teaspoon ground cumin

1 can (about 15 ounces) red kidney beans, rinsed and drained

¼ cup chopped fresh cilantro leaves

Chili Toppings: Chopped tomatoes, chopped onions **or** shredded cheese (optional)

1. Heat **1 tablespoon** of the oil in a 4-quart saucepan over medium-high heat. Add the beef in 2 batches and cook until it's well browned, stirring often. Remove the beef with a slotted spoon and set aside.

2. Reduce the heat to medium and add the remaining oil. Add the onion. Cook and stir until the onion is tender. Add the garlic and cook for 30 seconds.

3. Stir the salsa, water, chili powder, cumin and beans into the saucepan. Heat to a boil. Return the beef to the saucepan. Reduce the heat to low. Cover and cook for 1 hour. Uncover and cook for 30 minutes more or until the meat is fork-tender. Sprinkle with cilantro and serve with *Chili Toppings*, if desired.

Whip up a meal with just one pan to wash

Supper in a Skillet

2-Step Chicken 'n' Biscuits
Recipe on page 46

New Orleans Shrimp Toss

Makes: 4 servings
Prep: 10 minutes
Cook: 15 minutes

2 tablespoons vegetable oil

2 tablespoons lemon juice

1 tablespoon Worcestershire sauce

1 teaspoon Cajun seasoning

1 pound fresh large shrimp, shelled and deveined

1 medium onion, chopped (about ½ cup)

2 cloves garlic, minced

1 can (10¾ ounces) Campbell's® Condensed Cream of Chicken
   with Herbs Soup

½ cup milk

1 teaspoon paprika

   Cornbread **or** biscuits

2 tablespoons chopped fresh chives

1. Mix **1 tablespoon** of the oil, lemon juice, Worcestershire and Cajun seasoning in a medium bowl. Add the shrimp and toss lightly to coat.

2. Heat the remaining oil in a 10-inch skillet over medium-high heat. Add the onion and garlic. Cook and stir until the onion is tender.

3. Stir the soup, milk and paprika into the skillet. Heat to a boil. Add the shrimp mixture to the skillet and reduce the heat to low. Cover and cook for 5 minutes or until the shrimp turn pink. Serve with the cornbread and sprinkle with the chives.

Beefy Vegetable Skillet

Makes: 4 servings
Prep: 5 minutes
Cook: 20 minutes
Stand: 5 minutes

1 pound ground beef

1 medium onion, chopped (about ½ cup)

2 medium zucchini, cut into quarters lengthwise and sliced (about 2 cups)

1 can (about 14½ ounces) stewed tomatoes

2 cups Pepperidge Farm® Cubed Herb Seasoned Stuffing

2 tablespoons grated Parmesan cheese

1. Cook the beef and onion in a 10-inch skillet over medium-high heat until the beef is well browned, stirring frequently to break up meat. Pour off any fat.

2. Add the zucchini and tomatoes. Heat to a boil. Reduce the heat to low. Cover and cook for 5 minutes or until the zucchini is tender. Remove from the heat.

3. Stir the stuffing and cheese into the skillet and stir lightly to coat. Cover the skillet and remove from the heat. Let stand for 5 minutes. Serve with additional cheese, if desired.

Chicken & Stuffing Skillet

Makes: 4 servings
Prep: 5 minutes
Cook: 20 minutes

3 tablespoons butter

4 skinless, boneless chicken breast halves

1 box (6 ounces) Pepperidge Farm® One Step Chicken Flavored
   Stuffing Mix

1¼ cups water

1 can (10¾ ounces) Campbell's® Condensed Cream of Mushroom
   Soup (Regular **or** 98% Fat Free)

½ cup milk

½ cup shredded Cheddar cheese

1. Heat **1 tablespoon** of the butter in a 10-inch skillet over medium-high heat. Add the chicken and cook for 12 to 15 minutes or until the chicken is cooked through. Remove the chicken and set aside.

2. Prepare the stuffing in the skillet using the water and the remaining butter according to the package directions except let it stand for 2 minutes.

3. Return the chicken to the skillet and reduce the heat to medium. Stir the soup and milk in a small bowl and pour it over the chicken. Sprinkle with the cheese. Cover and cook until the mixture is hot and bubbling.

Southwest Skillet

Makes: 4 servings
Prep: 5 minutes
Cook: 20 minutes
Stand: 5 minutes

¾ pound ground beef

1 tablespoon chili powder

1 can (10¾ ounces) Campbell's® Condensed Beefy Mushroom Soup

¼ cup water

1 can (14½ ounces) whole peeled tomatoes, cut up

1 can (about 15 ounces) red kidney beans, rinsed and drained

¾ cup **uncooked** instant white rice

½ cup shredded Cheddar cheese

Tortilla chips

1. Cook the beef with chili powder in a 10-inch skillet over medium-high heat until the beef is well browned, stirring frequently to break up meat. Pour off any fat.

2. Stir the soup, water, tomatoes and beans into the skillet. Heat to a boil. Reduce the heat to low. Cover and cook for 10 minutes. Remove from the heat.

3. Stir the rice into the skillet. Cover the skillet and remove from the heat. Let stand for 5 minutes. Top with the cheese. Serve with the chips.

Zesty Turkey & Rice

Makes: 4 servings
Prep: 5 minutes
Cook: 30 minutes

1¾ cups Swanson® Chicken Broth (Regular, Natural Goodness™ **or** Certified Organic)

1 teaspoon dried basil leaves, crushed

¼ teaspoon garlic powder

¼ teaspoon hot pepper sauce

1 can (about 14½ ounces) stewed tomatoes

¾ cup **uncooked** regular long-grain white rice

2 cups cubed cooked turkey **or** chicken

1 cup frozen peas

1. Heat the broth, basil, garlic powder, hot pepper sauce and tomatoes in a 10-inch skillet over medium-high heat to a boil.

2. Stir in the rice. Reduce the heat to low. Cover the skillet and cook for 20 minutes.

3. Stir in the turkey and peas. Cover and cook for 5 minutes or until the rice is tender and most of the liquid is absorbed.

Sausage & Broccoli Skillet

Makes: 6 servings
Prep: 5 minutes
Cook: 20 minutes

1½ pounds sweet Italian pork sausage, casing removed

1 medium onion, chopped (about ½ cup)

2 cloves garlic, minced

1 can (10¾ ounces) Campbell's® Condensed Cream of Broccoli Soup (Regular **or** 98% Fat Free)

½ cup milk

1 bag (about 16 ounces) frozen broccoli cuts

½ cup shredded Parmesan cheese

4 cups corkscrew-shaped pasta (rotini), cooked and drained

Crushed red pepper (optional)

1. Cook the sausage in a 12-inch skillet over medium-high heat until it's well browned, stirring frequently to break up meat.

2. Reduce the heat to medium. Stir the onion and garlic into the skillet. Cook and stir until the onion is tender. Pour off any fat.

3. Stir the soup, milk, broccoli and ¼ **cup** of the cheese into the skillet. Heat to a boil. Reduce the heat to low. Cover and cook for 5 minutes or until the broccoli is tender, stirring occasionally.

4. Put the pasta in a large serving bowl. Pour the soup mixture over the pasta. Toss to coat. Sprinkle with the remaining cheese. Serve with red pepper, if desired.

Citrus Chicken and Rice

Makes: 4 servings
Prep: 5 minutes
Cook: 35 minutes

Vegetable cooking spray

4 skinless, boneless chicken breast halves

1¾ cups Swanson® Chicken Broth (Regular, Natural Goodness™ **or** Certified Organic)

½ cup orange juice

1 medium onion, chopped (about ½ cup)

1 cup **uncooked** regular long-grain white rice

3 tablespoons chopped fresh parsley **or** 1 tablespoon dried parsley flakes

Orange slices

1. Spray a 10-inch skillet with cooking spray and heat over medium-high heat for 1 minute. Add the chicken and cook for 10 minutes or until it's well browned on both sides. Remove the chicken and set aside.

2. Stir the broth, orange juice, onion and rice into the skillet. Heat to a boil. Reduce the heat to low. Cover and cook for 10 minutes.

3. Return the chicken to the skillet. Cover and cook for 10 minutes more or until chicken is cooked through. Stir in the parsley and top with the orange slices.

Pork Chop Skillet Dinner

Makes: 4 servings
Prep: 5 minutes
Cook: 40 minutes

1 tablespoon olive **or** vegetable oil

4 bone-in pork chops, ¾ inch thick

1 medium onion, chopped (about ½ cup)

1 cup **uncooked** regular long-grain white rice

1 can (10½ ounces) Campbell's® Condensed Chicken Broth

1 cup orange juice

3 tablespoons chopped fresh parsley

4 orange slices

1. Heat the oil in a 10-inch skillet over medium-high heat. Add the pork chops and cook for 10 minutes or until browned on both sides. Remove the pork chops and set aside.

2. Reduce the heat to medium. Stir the onion and rice into the skillet. Cook and stir until the rice is browned. Stir the broth, orange juice and **2 tablespoons** of the parsley into the skillet. Heat to a boil.

3. Return the pork chops to the skillet and reduce the heat to low. Cover and cook for 20 minutes or until the pork is cooked through and the rice is tender. Top with the orange slices and sprinkle with the remaining parsley.

Pasta with the Works

Makes: 4 servings
Prep: 5 minutes
Cook: 20 minutes

1 medium green pepper, cut into 2-inch-long strips (about 1½ cups)

½ cup thinly sliced pepperoni

2 cups Prego® Fresh Mushroom **or** Traditional Italian Sauce

⅓ cup pitted ripe olives, cut in half (optional)

3 cups corkscrew-shaped pasta (rotini), cooked and drained

1 cup shredded mozzarella cheese (4 ounces)

Grated Parmesan cheese

1. Cook the pepper and pepperoni in a 10-inch skillet over medium heat until the pepper is tender-crisp, stirring often.

2. Stir the Italian sauce and olives, if desired, into the skillet. Heat to a boil. Reduce the heat to low. Cover and cook for 10 minutes.

3. Stir in the pasta and mozzarella cheese. Serve with the Parmesan cheese.

Wild Mushroom Chicken Balsamico

Makes: 4 servings
Prep: 10 minutes
Cook: 30 minutes

3   teaspoons olive **or** vegetable oil

4   skinless, boneless chicken breast halves

12 ounces assorted wild mushrooms (portobello, shiitake, oyster **and/or** crimini), sliced (about 3 cups)

1   medium zucchini, sliced (about 1½ cups)

1   medium onion, cut into wedges

2   cloves garlic, minced

2   cups Prego® Marinara Italian Sauce

¼   cup balsamic vinegar

Freshly ground black pepper

1. Heat **1 teaspoon** of the oil in a 12-inch skillet over medium-high heat. Add the chicken and cook for 10 minutes or until it's well browned on both sides. Remove the chicken and set aside.

2. Reduce the heat to medium and add the remaining oil. Add the mushrooms, zucchini and onion. Cook and stir until tender. Add the garlic and cook for 1 minute.

3. Stir the Italian sauce and vinegar into the skillet. Heat to a boil. Return the chicken to the skillet and reduce the heat to low. Cover and cook for 10 minutes or until the chicken is cooked through. Serve with the black pepper.

Beef Taco Skillet

Makes: 4 servings
Prep: 5 minutes
Cook: 20 minutes

1 pound ground beef

1 can (10¾ ounces) Campbell's® Condensed Tomato Soup (Regular **or** Healthy Request®)

1 cup chunky salsa **or** picante sauce

½ cup water

8 corn **or** flour tortillas (6-inch), cut into 1-inch pieces

1 cup shredded Cheddar cheese (4 ounces)

1. Cook the beef in a 10-inch skillet over medium-high heat until the beef is well browned, stirring frequently to break up meat. Pour off any fat.

2. Stir the soup, salsa, water, tortillas and ½ **cup** of the cheese into the skillet. Heat to a boil. Reduce the heat to low. Cover and cook for 5 minutes or until hot and bubbling.

3. Top with the remaining cheese.

Chicken & Noodles

Makes: 4 servings
Prep: 10 minutes
Cook: 20 minutes

1 tablespoon vegetable oil

1 pound skinless, boneless chicken breasts, cut into cubes

1 can (10¾ ounces) Campbell's® Condensed Cream of Chicken Soup (Regular **or** 98% Fat Free)

½ cup milk

⅛ teaspoon ground black pepper

3 cups medium egg noodles, cooked and drained

⅓ cup grated Parmesan cheese

1. Heat the oil in a 10-inch skillet over medium-high heat. Add the chicken and cook until it's well browned, stirring often.

2. Stir the soup, milk, black pepper, noodles and cheese. Cook and stir until the mixture is hot and bubbling.

Cheesy Chicken and Rice

Cheesy Chicken and Rice

Makes: 4 servings
Prep: 5 minutes
Cook: 20 minutes

- 1 tablespoon vegetable oil
- 4 skinless, boneless chicken breast halves
- 1 can (10¾ ounces) Campbell's® Condensed Cream of Chicken Soup (Regular **or** 98% Fat Free)
- 1½ cups water
- ¼ teaspoon paprika
- ¼ teaspoon ground black pepper
- 2 cups fresh **or** frozen broccoli flowerets
- 1½ cups **uncooked** instant white rice
- ½ cup shredded Cheddar cheese

1. Heat the oil in a 10-inch skillet over medium-high heat. Add the chicken and cook for 10 minutes or until it's well browned on both sides. Remove the chicken and set aside.

2. Stir the soup, water, paprika and black pepper into the skillet. Heat to a boil.

3. Stir in the broccoli and rice. Return the chicken to the skillet and reduce the heat to low. Sprinkle the chicken with additional paprika and black pepper. Top with the cheese. Cover and cook for 5 minutes or until chicken is cooked through and the rice is tender.

Campbell's Kitchen Tip: For Cheesy Chicken & Rice Casserole *(pictured on front cover)*: Omit oil. Stir 1 can (10¾ ounces) Campbell's® Condensed Cream of Chicken Soup (Regular **or** 98% Fat Free), 1⅓ cups water, ¾ cup **uncooked** long-grain rice, 2 cups fresh **or** frozen vegetables, ½ teaspoon onion powder and ¼ teaspoon black pepper in a 11×8-inch (2-quart) shallow baking dish. Top with 4 skinless, boneless chicken breast halves, sprinkle with additional pepper. Cover. Bake at 375°F. for 45 minutes or until done. Top with cheese.

Chicken with White Beans

Makes: 4 servings
Prep: 10 minutes
Cook: 45 minutes

1   tablespoon vegetable oil

4   bone-in chicken breast halves (about 2 pounds)

2   cups Prego® Traditional Italian Sauce

¼   teaspoon garlic powder **or** 1 clove garlic, minced

1   large onion, chopped (about 1 cup)

2   cans (about 15 ounces **each**) white kidney (cannellini) beans, rinsed and drained

1. Heat the oil in a 10-inch skillet over medium-high heat. Add the chicken and cook for 10 minutes or until it's well browned.

2. Stir the Italian sauce, garlic powder, onion and beans into the skillet. Heat to a boil. Reduce the heat to low. Cover and cook for 30 minutes or until chicken is cooked through.

Lemon Asparagus Chicken

Makes: 4 servings
Prep: 5 minutes
Cook: 20 minutes

1 tablespoon vegetable oil

4 skinless, boneless chicken breast halves

1 can (10¾ ounces) Campbell's® Condensed Cream of
   Asparagus Soup

¼ cup milk

1 tablespoon lemon juice

⅛ teaspoon ground black pepper

1. Heat the oil in a 10-inch skillet over medium-high heat. Add chicken and cook for 10 minutes or until browned on both sides. Remove the chicken and set aside.

2. Stir the soup, milk, lemon juice and black pepper into the skillet. Heat to a boil. Return the chicken to the skillet and reduce the heat to low. Cover and cook for 5 minutes or until the chicken is cooked through.

Fast Fiesta Shepherd's Pie

Makes: 4 servings
Prep: 5 minutes
Cook: 15 minutes

1 pound ground beef

1 can (10¾ ounces) Campbell's® Condensed Tomato Soup (Regular **or** Healthy Request®)

¾ cup picante sauce

1 teaspoon ground cumin

1 cup frozen whole kernel corn

1 can (11 ounces) Campbell's® Condensed Fiesta Nacho Cheese Soup

1 cup milk

2 tablespoons butter

1⅓ cups instant mashed potato flakes **or** buds

Chopped fresh cilantro leaves **or** parsley (optional)

1. Cook the beef in a 10-inch skillet over medium-high heat until the beef is well browned, stirring frequently to break up meat. Pour off any fat.

2. Stir in the tomato soup, picante sauce, cumin and corn and heat to a boil. Reduce the heat to low and cook for 5 minutes, stirring occasionally.

3. Heat the cheese soup, milk and butter in a 2-quart saucepan over medium-high heat to a boil. Remove from the heat. Stir in the potato flakes. Let stand for 30 seconds. Mix with a fork until it's evenly moistened. Drop the potato mixture by large spoonfuls onto the beef mixture. Sprinkle with the cilantro, if desired.

Skillet Sausage and Stuffing

Makes: 4 servings
Prep: 10 minutes
Cook: 20 minutes
Stand: 5 minutes

  1 pound sweet **or** hot Italian pork sausage, cut into 1-inch pieces

1¼ cups water*

  1 medium onion, cut into wedges

  1 small green **or** red pepper, cut into 2-inch-long strips (about 1 cup)

  4 cups Pepperidge Farm® Herb Seasoned Stuffing

1. Cook the sausage in a 10-inch skillet over medium-high heat until it's well browned, stirring often. Pour off any fat.

2. Stir the water, onion and pepper into the skillet. Heat to a boil. Reduce the heat to low. Cover and cook for 5 minutes or until the sausage is cooked through.

3. Add the stuffing and stir lightly to coat. Remove from the heat. Cover and let stand for 5 minutes.

*For moister stuffing, increase water to 1½ **cups**.

Chicken & Roasted Garlic Risotto

Makes: 4 servings
Prep: 5 minutes
Cook: 20 minutes
Stand: 5 minutes

4 skinless, boneless chicken breast halves

1 tablespoon butter

1 can (10¾ ounces) Campbell's® Condensed Cream of Chicken Soup (Regular **or** 98% Fat Free)

1 can (10¾ ounces) Campbell's® Condensed Cream of Mushroom with Roasted Garlic Soup

2 cups water

2 cups **uncooked** instant white rice*

1 cup frozen peas and carrots

1. Season the chicken as desired.

2. Heat the butter in a 10-inch skillet over medium-high heat. Add the chicken and cook for 10 minutes or until it's well browned on both sides. Remove the chicken and set aside.

3. Stir the soups and water into the skillet. Heat to a boil. Stir in the rice and vegetables. Return the chicken to the skillet and reduce the heat to low. Cover and cook for 5 minutes or until the chicken is cooked through. Remove from the heat. Let stand for 5 minutes.

*For a creamier dish, use 1½ **cups** rice.

Shortcut Stroganoff

Makes: 4 servings
Prep: 5 minutes
Cook: 30 minutes

1 tablespoon vegetable oil

1 pound boneless beef sirloin steak, cut into thin strips

1 can (10¾ ounces) Campbell's® Condensed Cream of Mushroom Soup (Regular **or** 98% Fat Free)

1 can (10½ ounces) Campbell's® Condensed Beef Broth

1 cup water

2 teaspoons Worcestershire sauce

3 cups **uncooked** corkscrew-shaped pasta (rotini)

½ cup sour cream

1. Heat the oil in a 10-inch skillet over medium-high heat. Add the beef and cook until it's well browned, stirring often.

2. Stir the soup, broth, water, Worcestershire and pasta into the skillet. Heat to a boil. Reduce the heat to medium. Cook and stir for 15 minutes or until the pasta is tender but still firm. Stir in the sour cream. Cook until the mixture is hot.

Creamy Pesto Chicken & Bow Ties

Makes: 4 servings
Prep: 5 minutes
Cook: 15 minutes

- 2 tablespoons butter
- 1 pound skinless, boneless chicken breasts, cut into cubes
- 1 can (10¾ ounces) Campbell's® Condensed Cream of Chicken Soup (Regular **or** 98% Fat Free)
- ½ cup milk
- ½ cup prepared pesto sauce
- 3 cups bow tie-shaped pasta (farfalle), cooked and drained

1. Heat the butter in a 10-inch skillet over medium-high heat. Add the chicken and cook until it's well browned, stirring often.

2. Stir the soup, milk and pesto sauce into the skillet. Heat to a boil. Reduce the heat to low. Cover and cook for 5 minutes or until the chicken is cooked through. Stir in the pasta. Cook until it's hot.

Pork with Roasted Peppers & Potatoes

Makes: 4 servings
Prep: 10 minutes
Cook: 30 minutes

4 boneless pork chops, ½ inch thick

   Ground black pepper

1 tablespoon olive oil

4 medium red potatoes, (about 1 pound), cut into 1-inch pieces

1 medium onion, sliced (about ½ cup)

1 teaspoon dried oregano leaves, crushed

1 cup Swanson® Chicken Broth (Regular, Natural Goodness™
   or Certified Organic)

½ cup diced roasted sweet peppers

1. Season the pork chops with the black pepper.

2. Heat the oil in a 10-inch skillet over medium-high heat. Add the pork chops and cook for 10 minutes or until browned on both sides. Remove the pork chops and set aside.

3. Add the potatoes, onion and oregano. Cook and stir for 5 minutes or until browned.

4. Stir the broth and sweet peppers into the skillet. Heat to a boil. Return the pork chops to the skillet and reduce the heat to low. Cover and cook for 10 minutes or until the pork is cooked through.

Broccoli Chicken Potato Parmesan

Makes: 4 servings
Prep: 5 minutes
Cook: 20 minutes

2 tablespoons vegetable oil

1 pound small red potatoes, sliced ¼ inch thick

1 can (10¾ ounces) Campbell's® Condensed Broccoli Cheese Soup (Regular **or** 98% Fat Free)

½ cup milk

¼ teaspoon garlic powder

2 cups fresh **or** frozen broccoli flowerets

1 package (about 10 ounces) refrigerated cooked chicken breast strips

¼ cup grated Parmesan cheese

1. Heat the oil in a 10-inch skillet over medium heat. Add the potatoes. Cover and cook for 10 minutes, stirring occasionally.

2. Stir the soup, milk, garlic powder, broccoli and chicken into the skillet. Sprinkle with the cheese. Heat to a boil. Reduce the heat to low. Cover and cook for 5 minutes or until the potatoes are fork-tender.

The
World's

Fare

Easy global cuisine with the accent on flavor

West African Vegetable Stew

Makes: 6 servings
Prep: 15 minutes
Cook: 30 minutes

1 tablespoon vegetable oil

2 large onions, sliced (about 2 cups)

2 cloves garlic, minced

2 sweet potatoes (about 1½ pounds), peeled and cut in half lengthwise and sliced

1 large tomato, coarsely chopped (1½ cups)

1 can (10½ ounces) Campbell's® Condensed Chicken Broth

½ cup water

½ teaspoon **each** ground cinnamon **and** crushed red pepper

½ cup raisins

4 cups coarsely chopped fresh spinach leaves

1 can (about 15 ounces) chickpeas (garbanzo beans), rinsed and drained

Hot cooked rice **or** couscous (optional)

1. Heat the oil in a 4-quart saucepan over medium heat. Add the onions and garlic and cook until the onions are tender.

2. Add the potatoes and tomato. Cook and stir for 5 minutes.

3. Stir the broth, water, cinnamon, red pepper and raisins into the saucepan. Heat to a boil. Reduce the heat to low. Cover and cook for 15 minutes.

4. Stir in the spinach and chickpeas. Cook until hot. Serve over rice or couscous, if desired.

Chicken Cacciatore & Pasta

Makes: 4 servings
Prep: 10 minutes
Cook: 30 minutes

1 tablespoon vegetable oil

4 skinless, boneless chicken breast halves **or** 8 boneless chicken thighs, skin removed

1¾ cups Swanson® Chicken Broth (Regular, Natural Goodness™ **or** Certified Organic)

1 teaspoon dried oregano leaves, crushed

½ teaspoon garlic powder **or** 2 cloves garlic, minced

1 can (14 ounces) whole peeled tomatoes, undrained and cut up

1 small green pepper, cut into 2-inch-long strips (about 1 cup)

1 medium onion, cut into wedges

2½ cups **uncooked** medium shell-shaped pasta

1. Heat the oil in a 10-inch skillet over medium-high heat. Add the chicken and cook for 10 minutes or until it's well browned on both sides.

2. Stir the broth, oregano, garlic powder, tomatoes, pepper and onion into the skillet. Heat to a boil. Stir in the pasta. Reduce the heat to low. Cover and cook for 15 minutes or until pasta is tender but still firm, stirring occasionally.

Easy Enchilada-Style Casserole

Makes: 8 servings
Prep Time: 10 minutes
Bake Time: 35 minutes

2 cans (10¾ ounces **each**) Campbell's® Condensed Cheddar Cheese Soup

½ cup water

1 jar (16 ounces) chunky salsa

4 cups cubed cooked chicken

8 flour **or** 12 corn tortillas (6- to 8-inch), cut into strips

1 cup shredded Cheddar cheese (4 ounces)

1. Mix the soup, water, ½ **cup** salsa and chicken in a 3-quart bowl. Stir in the tortillas. Spread the chicken mixture in a 13×9×2-inch (3-quart) shallow baking dish. Top with the cheese. **Cover.**

2. Bake at 350°F. for 35 minutes or until hot and bubbly. Serve with the remaining salsa.

Mediterranean Chicken & Rice Bake

Makes: 6 servings
Prep: 10 minutes
Bake: 50 minutes

1¾ cups Swanson® Chicken Broth (Regular, Natural Goodness™
   or Certified Organic)

¼ cup chopped fresh parsley

¼ cup sliced pitted ripe olives

1 tablespoon fresh lemon juice

¼ teaspoon ground black pepper

1 can (about 14½ ounces) stewed tomatoes

1¼ cups **uncooked** regular long-grain white rice

6 skinless, boneless chicken breast halves

½ teaspoon garlic powder

Paprika

1. Stir the broth, parsley, olives, lemon juice, black pepper, tomatoes and rice in a 13×9×2-inch (3-quart) shallow baking dish. **Cover.**

2. Bake at 375°F. for 20 minutes.

3. Place the chicken on the rice mixture. Sprinkle with garlic powder and paprika. Bake for 30 minutes more or until the chicken is cooked through and the rice is tender.

Zesty Rice with Chorizo

Makes: 4 servings
Prep: 10 minutes
Cook: 30 minutes

- 1 tablespoon vegetable oil
- 1 package (3½ ounces) chorizo sausage, cut into cubes
- 1 medium onion, chopped (about ½ cup)
- 2 cloves garlic, minced
- 1¾ cups Swanson® Chicken Broth (Regular, Natural Goodness™ **or** Certified Organic)
- ½ cup chunky salsa
- ¾ cup **uncooked** regular long-grain white rice
- ½ cup frozen peas

  Chopped fresh cilantro leaves (optional)

1. Heat the oil in a 10-inch skillet over medium-high heat. Add the sausage, onion and garlic and cook until the onion is tender.

2. Stir the broth, salsa and rice into the skillet. Heat to a boil. Reduce the heat to low. Cover and cook for 15 minutes.

3. Stir in the peas. Cover and cook for 5 minutes more or until the rice is tender and most of the liquid is absorbed. Sprinkle with the cilantro, if desired.

Easy Substitution Tip: Use chipotle chunky salsa for the regular salsa.

Italian-Style Pot Roast

Makes: 8 servings
Prep: 5 minutes
Cook: 3 hours
Stand: 10 minutes

2 tablespoons vegetable oil

   3½- to 4-pound boneless beef bottom round **or** chuck
     pot roast

1 jar (1 pound 10 ounces) Prego® Traditional Italian Sauce

6 medium potatoes (about 1½ pounds), cut into quarters

6 medium carrots (about ¾ pound), cut into 2-inch pieces

1. Heat the oil in a 6-quart saucepot. Add the roast and cook until browned on all sides. Pour off any fat.

2. Pour the Italian sauce into the saucepot. Heat to a boil. Reduce the heat to low. Cover and cook for 1 hour 45 minutes.

3. Add the potatoes and carrots. Cover and cook for 1 hour more or until the meat and vegetables are fork-tender.

4. Remove the roast to a cutting board and let it stand for 10 minutes before slicing. Thinly slice the roast and arrange on a serving platter. Remove the vegetables with a slotted spoon and put on platter. Pour the sauce mixture into a gravy boat and serve with the roast and vegetables.

Moroccan Lamb Stew

Makes: 8 servings
Prep: 15 minutes
Cook: 1 hour 35 minutes

1 tablespoon olive oil

2 pounds lamb for stew, cut into 1-inch pieces

½ teaspoon ground cinnamon

¼ teaspoon ground cloves

1 medium onion, chopped (about ½ cup)

4 cups Swanson® Chicken Broth (Regular, Natural Goodness™ **or** Certified Organic)

1 cup dried lentils

2 medium potatoes, cut into cubes (about 2 cups)

Hot cooked couscous (optional)

Chopped fresh cilantro leaves (optional)

1. Heat the oil in a 6-quart saucepot over medium-high heat. Add the lamb in 2 batches and cook until it's well browned, stirring often. Remove the lamb with a slotted spoon and put in a medium bowl. Sprinkle the cinnamon and cloves over the lamb and stir to coat.

2. Reduce the heat to medium. Add the onion and cook until tender-crisp.

3. Stir the broth into the saucepot. Heat to a boil. Return the lamb to the saucepot and reduce the heat to low. Cover and cook for 1 hour.

4. Add the lentils and potatoes. Cook for 20 minutes more or until the lentils and potatoes are tender. Serve over the couscous and sprinkle with the cilantro, if desired.

Mexican Lasagna

Makes: 8 servings
Prep: 20 minutes
Cook: 10 minutes
Bake: 20 minutes
Stand: 5 minutes

1 pound ground beef

1 large green pepper, chopped (about 1 cup)

2 cups Prego® Traditional Italian Sauce

1½ cups picante sauce

1 tablespoon chili powder

8 flour tortillas (6-inch)

2 cups shredded Cheddar cheese (8 ounces)

2 cans (2¼ ounces **each**) sliced pitted ripe olives, drained

1. Cook the beef and pepper in a 10-inch skillet over medium-high heat until the beef is well browned, stirring frequently to break up meat. Pour off any fat.

2. Stir the Italian sauce, **1 cup** of the picante sauce and chili powder into the skillet. Heat to a boil. Reduce the heat to low. Cook for 10 minutes.

3. Spread the remaining picante sauce in a 13×9×2-inch (3-quart) shallow baking dish. Arrange **4** tortillas in the dish. Top with **half** of the beef mixture, **1 cup** of the cheese and **half** of the olives. Repeat the layers.

4. Bake at 350°F. for 20 minutes or until hot. Let the lasagna stand for 5 minutes before serving.

Easy Substitution Tip: Substitute **1 pound** skinless, boneless chicken breast halves, cut into cubes, for the ground beef.

Spicy Salsa Mac & Beef

Makes: 4 servings
Prep: 5 minutes
Cook: 20 minutes

- 1 pound ground beef
- 1 can (10½ ounces) Campbell's® Condensed Beef Broth
- 1⅓ cups water
- 2 cups **uncooked** medium shell-shaped pasta
- 1 can (10¾ ounces) Campbell's® Condensed Cheddar Cheese Soup
- 1 cup chunky salsa

1. Cook the beef in a 10-inch skillet over medium-high heat until the beef is well browned, stirring frequently to break up meat. Pour off any fat.

2. Stir the broth and water into the skillet. Heat to a boil. Add the pasta. Reduce the heat to medium. Cook and stir for 10 minutes or until the pasta is tender but still firm.

3. Stir the soup and salsa into the skillet. Cook and stir until hot and bubbling.

Steak & Mushroom Florentine

Makes: 4 servings
Prep: 10 minutes
Cook: 20 minutes

2 tablespoons vegetable oil

1 pound boneless beef sirloin **or** top round steak, ¾ inch thick, cut into thin strips

1 small onion, sliced (about ¼ cup)

4 cups baby spinach leaves, washed

1 can (10¾ ounces) Campbell's® Condensed Cream of Mushroom Soup (Regular **or** 98% Fat Free)

1 cup water

1 large tomato, thickly sliced

Freshly ground black pepper

1. Heat **1 tablespoon** of the oil in a 10-inch skillet over medium-high heat. Add the beef and cook until it's well browned, stirring often. Remove the beef with a slotted spoon and set aside.

2. Heat the remaining oil over medium heat. Add the onion and cook until tender-crisp. Add the spinach and cook just until the spinach wilts.

3. Stir the soup and water into the skillet. Heat to a boil. Return the beef to the skillet and reduce the heat to low. Cook until the beef is cooked through. Serve the beef mixture with the tomato. Season to taste with black pepper.

Asian Chicken & Rice Bake

Makes: 4 servings
Prep: 5 minutes
Bake: 45 minutes

¾ cup **uncooked** regular long-grain white rice

4 skinless, boneless chicken breast halves

1 can (10¾ ounces) Campbell's® Condensed Golden Mushroom Soup

¾ cup water

2 tablespoons soy sauce

2 tablespoons cider vinegar

2 tablespoons honey

1 teaspoon garlic powder

Paprika

1. Spread the rice in an 11×8-inch (2-quart) shallow baking dish. Top with the chicken.

2. Stir the soup, water, soy sauce, vinegar, honey and garlic powder in a medium bowl. Pour the soup mixture over the chicken. Sprinkle with paprika. **Cover.**

3. Bake at 375°F. for 45 minutes or until the chicken is cooked through.

Campbell's Kitchen Tip: Add 2 cups frozen broccoli flowerets to the rice before baking. Serve with your favorite stir-fry vegetable blend.

Jollof Chicken & Rice

Makes: 4 servings
Prep: 15 minutes
Cook: 45 minutes
Stand: 5 minutes

1   tablespoon vegetable oil

2½- to 3½-pound broiler-fryer chicken, cut up

1   large onion, chopped (about 1 cup)

2   cloves garlic, minced

4   plum tomatoes, coarsely chopped (about 2 cups)

1   can (10½ ounces) Campbell's® Condensed Chicken Broth

½   cup water

½   teaspoon crushed red pepper

Few saffron threads **or** ¼ teaspoon ground turmeric

1   cup **uncooked** regular long-grain white rice

1   cup coarsely chopped fresh spinach leaves

1. Heat the oil in a 12-inch skillet over medium-high heat. Add the chicken and cook for 10 minutes or until it's well browned on all sides. Remove the chicken.

2. Reduce the heat to medium. Add the onion and garlic and cook until tender. Add the tomatoes and cook for 2 minutes.

3. Stir the broth, water, red pepper, saffron and rice into the skillet. Heat to a boil. Return the chicken to skillet and reduce the heat to low. Cover and cook for 25 minutes or until the chicken is cooked through.

4. Stir in the spinach. Let stand for 5 minutes.

Surefire shortcuts to favorite family standards

Quick & Easy
Classics

Quick Chicken Parmesan

Makes: 4 servings
Prep: 5 minutes
Bake: 10 minutes

2 cups Prego® Traditional Italian Sauce

4 fully cooked breaded chicken cutlets

4 thin slices cooked ham

1 cup shredded mozzarella cheese (4 ounces)

2 tablespoons grated Parmesan cheese

1. Spread **1 cup** of the Italian sauce in an 11×8-inch (2-quart) shallow baking dish.

2. Place the chicken cutlets over the sauce. Spoon ¼ **cup** of the remaining sauce down the center of each cutlet. Top each with **1 slice** ham and ¼ **cup** of the mozzarella cheese. Sprinkle with the Parmesan cheese.

3. Bake at 425°F. for 10 minutes or until the cheese melts and the sauce is hot and bubbly.

Chicken & Biscuits Casserole

Makes: 5 servings
Prep: 10 minutes
Bake: 30 minutes

1 can (10¾ ounces) Campbell's® Condensed Cream of Celery Soup (Regular **or** 98% Fat Free)

1 can (10¾ ounces) Campbell's® Condensed Cream of Potato Soup

1 cup milk

¼ teaspoon dried thyme leaves, crushed

¼ teaspoon ground black pepper

4 cups cooked cut-up vegetables*

2 cups cubed cooked chicken

1 package (about 7 ounces) refrigerated buttermilk biscuits (10)

1. Stir the soups, milk, thyme, black pepper, vegetables and chicken in a 13×9×2-inch (3-quart) shallow baking dish.

2. Bake at 400°F. for 15 minutes. Stir.

3. Cut each biscuit into quarters. Arrange cut biscuits over the chicken mixture.

4. Bake for 15 minutes more or until the biscuits are golden.

Use a combination of broccoli flowerets, cauliflower flowerets and carrots.

Miracle Lasagna

Makes: 10 servings
Prep: 5 minutes
Bake: 1 hour
Stand: 5 minutes

1 jar (48 ounces) Prego® Traditional Italian Sauce

12 **uncooked** lasagna noodles

2 containers (15 ounces **each**) ricotta cheese

2 cups shredded mozzarella cheese (8 ounces)

6 tablespoons grated Parmesan cheese

1. Spread about **1 cup** of the sauce in a 13×9×2-inch (3-quart) shallow baking dish. Top with **3** noodles, **1 cup** of the ricotta cheese, ½ **cup** of the mozzarella cheese, **2 tablespoons** of the Parmesan cheese and **1 cup** of the sauce. Repeat the layers twice. Top with the remaining **3** noodles and the remaining sauce. **Cover.**

2. Bake at 375°F. for 1 hour or until hot and bubbly. Uncover and top with the remaining mozzarella cheese. Let the lasagna stand for 5 minutes before serving.

Easy Chicken Pot Pie

Makes: 4 servings
Prep: 5 minutes
Bake: 30 minutes

1 can (10¾ ounces) Campbell's® Condensed Cream of Chicken
    Soup (Regular **or** 98% Fat Free)

1 package (about 9 ounces) frozen mixed vegetables, thawed

1 cup cubed cooked chicken **or** turkey

1 cup all-purpose baking mix

1 egg

½ cup milk

1. Heat the oven to 400°F.

2. Stir the soup, vegetables and chicken in a 9-inch pie plate.

3. Stir together the baking mix, egg and milk with a fork to form a
soft dough. Pour over the chicken mixture.

4. Bake for 30 minutes or until the topping is golden brown.

Southern Cornbread Turkey Pot Pie

Makes: 4 servings
Prep: 10 minutes
Cook: 5 minutes
Bake: 15 minutes

1 can (10¾ ounces) Campbell's® Condensed Cream of Chicken Soup (Regular **or** 98% Fat Free)

⅛ teaspoon ground black pepper

1 can (about 8 ounces) whole kernel corn, drained

2 cups cubed cooked turkey **or** chicken

1 package (11 ounces) refrigerated cornbread twists **or** breadsticks

1. Heat the oven to 425°F.

2. Stir the soup, black pepper, corn and turkey in a 2-quart saucepan over medium heat. Cook and stir until it's hot. Pour the turkey mixture into a 9-inch pie plate.

3. Separate cornbread into 8 pieces along perforations. (Do not unroll dough.) Place over hot turkey mixture.

4. Bake for 15 minutes or until bread is golden.

Pork & Corn Stuffing Bake

Makes: 4 servings
Prep: 10 minutes
Bake: 30 minutes

Vegetable cooking spray

1½ cups Pepperidge Farm® Corn Bread Stuffing **or** Herb Seasoned Stuffing

1 can (10¾ ounces) Campbell's® Condensed Cream of Celery Soup (Regular **or** 98% Fat Free)

½ cup whole kernel corn

1 small onion, finely chopped (about ¼ cup)

¼ cup finely chopped celery

4 boneless pork chops, ¾ inch thick

1 tablespoon packed brown sugar

1 teaspoon spicy-brown mustard

1. Spray a 9-inch pie plate with cooking spray. Stir the stuffing, soup, corn, onion and celery in a medium bowl. Spoon the stuffing mixture into the prepared dish. Top with the pork chops.

2. Stir the brown sugar and mustard in a small cup. Spoon over the pork chops.

3. Bake at 400°F. for 30 minutes or until the chops are cooked through.

Savory Pot Roast & Harvest Vegetables

Makes: 6 servings
Prep: 15 minutes
Cook: 2 hours 30 minutes

2   tablespoons vegetable oil

   3-pound boneless beef bottom round **or** chuck pot roast

1¾   cups Swanson® Seasoned Beef Broth with Onion

¾   cup V8® 100% Vegetable Juice

3   medium potatoes (about ¾ pound), cut into quarters

3   stalks celery, cut into 1-inch pieces (about 2¼ cups)

2   cups fresh **or** frozen baby carrots

2   tablespoons all-purpose flour

¼   cup water

1. Heat the oil in a 4-quart saucepan over medium-high heat. Add the roast and cook until it's well browned on all sides. Pour off any fat.

2. Add the broth and vegetable juice to the saucepan. Heat to a boil. Reduce the heat to low. Cover and cook for 1 hour 45 minutes.

3. Add the potatoes, celery and carrots. Cover and cook for 30 minutes more or until the meat and vegetables are fork-tender.

4. Remove the roast to a cutting board and let it stand for 10 minutes before slicing. Remove the vegetables with a slotted spoon and arrange on a serving platter. Slice the roast and put on platter.

5. Stir the flour and water in a small cup and stir into the broth mixture. Cook and stir over medium-high heat until the mixture boils and thickens. Pour the gravy into a gravy boat and serve with the roast and vegetables.

Easy Substitution Tip: Substitute Calcium Enriched V8® **or** 100% Vitamins A, C & E Healthy Request® V8® for the 100% Vegetable Juice.

Sausage-Stuffed Green Peppers

Makes: 8 servings
Prep: 10 minutes
Cook: 10 minutes
Bake: 40 minutes

4　medium green peppers

1　tablespoon vegetable oil

1　pound sweet Italian pork sausage, casing removed

1　teaspoon dried oregano leaves, crushed

1　medium onion, chopped (about ½ cup)

1　cup shredded part-skim mozzarella cheese (4 ounces)

2　cups Prego® Traditional Italian Sauce

1. Cut a thin slice from the top of each pepper, cut in half lengthwise and discard the seeds and white membranes. Place the pepper shells in a 3-quart casserole **or** a 13×9×2-inch (3-quart) shallow baking dish and set them aside.

2. Heat the oil in a 10-inch skillet over medium-high heat. Add the sausage and cook until it's well browned, stirring to break up the meat. Add the oregano and onion and cook until the onion is tender. Pour off any fat. Stir in the cheese.

3. Spoon the sausage mixture into the pepper shells. Pour the Italian sauce over the peppers. **Cover.**

4. Bake at 400°F. for 40 minutes or until sausage is cooked through and the peppers are tender.

Easy Beef Pot Pie

Makes: 4 servings
Prep: 15 minutes
Bake: 35 minutes

½ of a 15-ounce package refrigerated pie crusts (1 crust)

2 cups diced cooked potatoes

1 package (10 ounces) frozen mixed vegetables, thawed (about 2 cups)

1½ cups diced cooked beef

1 can (10¾ ounces) Campbell's® Condensed Golden Mushroom Soup

⅓ cup water

1 teaspoon Worcestershire sauce

1 teaspoon dried thyme leaves, crushed

1. Heat the oven to 400°F. Let the pie crust stand at room temperature for 15 minutes or until it's easy to handle.

2. Put the potatoes, vegetables and beef in a 9-inch deep-dish pie plate or 1½-quart shallow baking dish.

3. Stir the soup, water, Worcestershire and thyme in a medium bowl. Pour the soup mixture over the beef mixture. Gently put the pie crust over the beef mixture. Crimp or roll the edges to seal it to the dish. Cut slits in the crust with a knife.

4. Bake for 35 minutes or until hot and the crust is golden brown.

Time-Saving Tip: To thaw the vegetables, microwave on HIGH for 3 minutes.

Green Bean Casserole

Makes: 6 servings
Prep: 10 minutes
Bake: 30 minutes

1 can (10¾ ounces) Campbell's® Condensed Cream of
   Mushroom Soup (Regular **or** 98% Fat Free)

½ cup milk

1 teaspoon soy sauce

   Dash ground black pepper

4 cups cooked cut green beans

1½ cups French fried onions

1. Stir the soup, milk, soy sauce, black pepper, green beans and ⅔ **cup** of the onions in a 1½-quart casserole.

2. Bake at 350°F. for 25 minutes or until hot. Stir the green bean mixture.

3. Sprinkle the remaining onions over the green bean mixture. Bake for 5 minutes more or until onions are golden brown.

Easy Substitution Tip: You can make this classic side dish with frozen, canned **or** fresh green beans. You will need either 1 bag (16 to 20 ounces) frozen green beans **or** 2 cans (about 16 ounces **each**) cut green beans, drained **or** about 1½ pounds fresh green beans for this recipe.

Tuna & Pasta Cheddar Melt

Makes: 4 servings
Prep: 5 minutes
Cook: 20 minutes

1 can (10½ ounces) Campbell's® Condensed Chicken Broth

1 soup can water

3 cups **uncooked** corkscrew-shaped pasta (rotini)

1 can (10¾ ounces) Campbell's® Condensed Cream of
    Mushroom Soup (Regular **or** 98% Fat Free)

1 cup milk

1 can (about 6 ounces) tuna, drained and flaked

1 cup shredded Cheddar cheese (4 ounces)

2 tablespoons Italian-seasoned dry bread crumbs

2 teaspoons butter, melted

1. Heat the broth and water in a 10-inch skillet over high heat to a boil. Add the pasta. Reduce the heat to medium. Cook and stir until the pasta is tender but still firm. Do not drain.

2. Stir the soup, milk and tuna into the skillet. Top with the cheese. Mix the bread crumbs with the butter in a small cup. Sprinkle the crumb mixture over the tuna mixture. Cook until the mixture is hot and bubbling.

Chicken Broccoli Divan

Makes: 4 servings
Prep: 15 minutes
Bake: 25 minutes

1 pound fresh broccoli, cut into spears **or** 1 package (about 10 ounces) frozen broccoli spears, cooked and drained

1½ cups cubed cooked chicken **or** turkey

1 can (10¾ ounces) Campbell's® Condensed Broccoli Cheese Soup (Regular **or** 98% Fat Free)

⅓ cup milk

½ cup shredded Cheddar cheese (optional)

2 tablespoons dry bread crumbs

1 tablespoon butter, melted

1. Arrange the broccoli and chicken in an 11×8-inch (2-quart) shallow baking dish.

2. Stir the soup and milk in a small bowl and pour over the broccoli and chicken mixture. Sprinkle the cheese, if desired, over the soup mixture. Mix the bread crumbs with the butter in a small cup. Sprinkle over the chicken mixture.

3. Bake at 400°F. for 25 minutes or until hot and bubbly.

Easy Substitution Tip: Substitute 1 can (10¾ ounces) Campbell's® Condensed Cream of Chicken Soup (Regular **or** 98% Fat Free) for the Broccoli Cheese Soup.

Tip: For 1½ **cups** cubed cooked chicken, cook ¾ **pound** skinless, boneless chicken breasts, cut into cubes, in a 2-quart saucepan over medium heat, in **4 cups** boiling water for 5 minutes or until the chicken is cooked through.

Super Bowl Chili Beans & Rice

Makes: 8 servings
Prep: 10 minutes
Cook: 35 minutes

Vegetable cooking spray

1½ pounds skinless, boneless chicken breasts, cut into cubes

1¾ cups Swanson® Chicken Broth (Regular, Natural Goodness™ **or** Certified Organic)

2 tablespoons chili powder

2 medium tomatoes, chopped (about 2 cups)

1 medium green pepper, chopped (about ¾ cup)

1 cup **uncooked** regular long-grain white rice

2 cans (16 ounces **each**) Campbell's® Pork & Beans

½ cup fat-free sour cream

Sliced green onions (optional)

1. Spray a 6-quart saucepot with cooking spray and heat over medium-high heat for 1 minute. Add the chicken in 2 batches and cook until it's well browned, stirring often.

2. Stir the broth, chili powder, tomatoes, pepper, rice and beans into the saucepot. Heat to a boil. Reduce the heat to low. Cover and cook for 20 minutes or until the rice is tender. Top with the sour cream and green onions, if desired.

25-Minute Chicken & Noodles

Makes: 4 servings
Prep: 5 minutes
Cook: 20 minutes

1¾ cups Swanson® Chicken Broth (Regular, Natural Goodness™
   or Certified Organic)

½ teaspoon dried basil leaves, crushed

⅛ teaspoon ground black pepper

2 cups frozen vegetable combination (broccoli, cauliflower,
   carrots)

2 cups **uncooked** medium egg noodles

2 cups cubed cooked chicken

1. Heat the broth, basil, black pepper and vegetables in a 10-inch
skillet over high heat to a boil. Reduce the heat to low. Cover and
cook for 5 minutes.

2. Stir the noodles into the skillet. Cover and cook for 5 minutes
more. Add the chicken. Cook and stir until hot.

Shortcut Beef Stew

Makes: 4 servings
Prep: 5 minutes
Cook: 20 minutes

1 tablespoon vegetable oil

1 pound boneless beef sirloin steak, ¾ inch thick, cut into 1-inch pieces

1 can (10¾ ounces) Campbell's® Condensed Tomato Soup (Regular **or** Healthy Request®)

1 can (10½ ounces) Campbell's® Condensed French Onion Soup

1 tablespoon Worcestershire sauce

1 bag (24 ounces) frozen vegetables for stew (potatoes, carrots, celery)

1. Heat the oil in a 10-inch skillet over medium-high heat. Add the beef and cook until it's well browned, stirring often.

2. Stir the soups, Worcestershire and vegetables into the skillet. Heat to a boil. Reduce the heat to low. Cover and cook for 10 minutes or until the vegetables are tender.

Easy Substitution Tip: Substitute 5 cups frozen vegetables (carrots, small whole onions, cut green beans, cauliflower, zucchini, peas or lima beans) for the frozen vegetables for stew.

Slow Cooker
Recipes

Contents

200

254

276

Slow cooking is the fastest way
to save time in the kitchen

Time
to

Many cooks have already discovered that using a slow cooker is the fastest way to get a home-cooked meal on the table, especially on hectic weeknights! That may sound like a contradiction, but saving time—and giving you extra time to savor—is the best benefit of slow cooking.

Preparation is usually pretty simple. You can even do most of it the night before. Assemble the ingredients (either in the crockery liner of your slow cooker or in a bowl), cover and store overnight in the refrigerator. In the morning, simply pop the ingredients into the slow cooker and set it before you set off on your busy day.

Cooking in the slow cooker also requires minimal attention. No supervising, no stirring, no scorching—just the pleasure of coming home to a home-cooked meal that's piping hot and ready to serve. It's also exceptionally delicious; because there's nothing like the slow cooker for mingling flavors and creating something really worth savoring. Thanks to the ease and convenience of the slow cooker, you'll have plenty of time to do just that!

Savor

Chicken in Creamy
Sun-Dried Tomato Sauce
Recipe on page 198

No-wait meals for busy weeknights
Supper's Ready

It's 6:00 p.m. The whole family—ravenously hungry and ready to eat—is finally home, including the chef (you), who just walked in the door along with everyone else. Good thing you thought ahead and started your slow cooker in the morning. What a fast, easy way to say "supper's ready!"

Slow cooking lends itself especially well to meal-in-one recipes that only require the addition of a salad and some bread or rolls to round out the menu—like this collection of ten easy weeknight dishes. While you go about your business during the day, your slow cooker is hard at work. So as soon as you return, there's a satisfying supper waiting that's ready when you are.

Chicken in Creamy Sun-Dried Tomato Sauce

(photo on page 196)

Makes: 8 servings
Prep: 15 minutes
Cook: 7 to 8 hours

2 cans (10¾ ounces **each**) Campbell's® Condensed Cream of Chicken Soup with Herbs

1 cup Chablis **or** other dry white wine

¼ cup coarsely chopped pitted kalamata **or** oil-cured olives

2 tablespoons capers, drained

2 cloves garlic, minced

1 can (14 ounces) artichoke hearts, drained and chopped

1 cup drained, coarsely chopped sun-dried tomatoes

8 skinless, boneless chicken breast halves

½ cup chopped fresh basil leaves (optional)

Hot cooked rice, egg noodles **or** seasoned mashed potatoes

1. Stir the soup, wine, olives, capers, garlic, artichokes and tomatoes in a 3½-quart slow cooker. Add the chicken and turn to coat with the soup mixture.

2. Cover and cook on LOW for 7 to 8 hours* or until the chicken is cooked through. Sprinkle with the basil, if desired. Serve with rice, noodles or potatoes.

Or on HIGH for 4 to 5 hours

Easy Substitution Tip: Substitute Swanson® Chicken Broth (Regular, Natural Goodness™ **or** Certified Organic) for the wine.

Weekday Pot Roast & Vegetables

Makes: 6 to 8 servings
Prep: 5 minutes
Cook: 10 to 12 hours 10 minutes
Stand: 10 minutes

2- to 2½-pound boneless beef bottom round **or** chuck pot roast

1 teaspoon garlic powder

1 tablespoon vegetable oil

4 medium potatoes (about 1 pound), each cut into 6 wedges

3 cups fresh **or** frozen baby carrots

1 medium onion, thickly sliced (about ¾ cup)

2 teaspoons dried basil leaves, crushed

2 cans (10¼ ounces **each**) Campbell's® Beef Gravy

1. Sprinkle all sides of the roast with the garlic powder. Heat the oil in a 10-inch skillet over medium-high heat. Add the roast and cook until it's browned on all sides.

2. Put the potatoes, carrots and onion in a 3½-quart slow cooker. Sprinkle with the basil. Top with the roast. Pour the gravy over the roast and vegetables.

3. Cover and cook on LOW for 10 to 12 hours* or until the meat is fork-tender.

4. Remove the roast to a cutting board and let it stand for 10 minutes before slicing. Thinly slice the roast and arrange on a serving platter. Remove the vegetables with a slotted spoon and put on platter. Pour the gravy into a gravy boat and serve with the roast and vegetables.

Or on HIGH for 5 to 6 hours

Campbell's Kitchen Tip: Browning the meat on the stovetop before adding it to the slow cooker adds to the flavor and color of the dish.

Slow-Cooked Pulled Pork Sandwiches

Makes: 12 sandwiches
Prep: 55 minutes
Cook: 8 to 10 hours 10 minutes
Stand: 10 minutes

  1 tablespoon vegetable oil

  3½- to 4-pound boneless pork shoulder roast, netted **or** tied

  1 can (10½ ounces) Campbell's® Condensed French Onion Soup

  1 cup ketchup

  ¼ cup cider vinegar

  3 tablespoons packed brown sugar

  12 round sandwich rolls, split

1. Heat the oil in a 10-inch skillet over medium-high heat. Add the roast and cook until it's well browned on all sides.

2. Stir the soup, ketchup, vinegar and brown sugar in a 5-quart slow cooker. Add the roast and turn to coat with the soup mixture.

3. Cover and cook on LOW for 8 to 10 hours* or until the meat is fork-tender.

4. Remove the roast from the cooker to a cutting board and let it stand for 10 minutes. Using 2 forks, shred the pork. Return the shredded pork to the cooker.

5. Divide the pork and sauce mixture among the rolls.

Or on HIGH for 4 to 5 hours

Serving Suggestion Tip: Complement this Southern-style sandwich favorite with store-bought cole slaw and dill pickles.

Orange Chicken with Green Onions & Walnuts

Makes: 8 servings
Prep: 10 minutes
Cook: 8 to 9 hours

2   tablespoons cornstarch

1½ cups Swanson® Chicken Broth (Regular, Natural Goodness™ **or** Certified Organic)

¼   cup teriyaki sauce

3   cloves garlic, minced

¾   cup orange marmalade

4   medium green onions, sliced (about ½ cup)

8   skinless chicken thighs (about 2 pounds)

½   cup walnut pieces

    Hot cooked rice

1. Stir the cornstarch, broth, teriyaki sauce, garlic, marmalade and ¼ **cup** of the green onions in a 6-quart slow cooker. Add the chicken and turn to coat with the broth mixture.

2. Cover and cook on LOW for 8 to 9 hours* or until the chicken is cooked through. Sprinkle with walnuts and remaining green onions before serving. Serve with rice.

Or on HIGH for 4 to 5 hours

Campbell's Kitchen Tip: Resist peeking! Every time the slow cooker lid is lifted, heat escapes—and 15 to 20 minutes will need to be added to the total cooking time.

Golden Chicken with Noodles

Makes: 8 servings
Prep: 5 minutes
Cook: 7 to 8 hours

2 cans (10¾ ounces **each**) Campbell's® Condensed Cream of Chicken Soup (Regular **or** 98% Fat Free)

½ cup water

¼ cup lemon juice

1 tablespoon Dijon-style mustard

1½ teaspoons garlic powder

8 large carrots, thickly sliced (about 6 cups)

8 skinless, boneless chicken breast halves

Hot cooked egg noodles

Chopped fresh parsley

1. Stir the soup, water, lemon juice, mustard, garlic powder and carrots in a 3½-quart slow cooker. Add the chicken and turn to coat with the soup mixture.

2. Cover and cook on LOW for 7 to 8 hours* or until the chicken is cooked through. Serve with noodles. Sprinkle with parsley.

Or on HIGH for 4 to 5 hours

Campbell's Kitchen Tip: Colors in slow-cooked food tend to fade, so add garnishes such as chopped fresh parsley just before serving.

Golden Mushroom Pork & Apples

Makes: 8 servings
Prep: 10 minutes
Cook: 8 to 9 hours

2 cans (10¾ ounces **each**) Campbell's® Condensed Golden Mushroom Soup

½ cup water

1 tablespoon packed brown sugar

1 tablespoon Worcestershire sauce

1 teaspoon dried thyme leaves, crushed

8 boneless pork chops, ¾ inch thick

4 large Granny Smith apples, sliced (about 6 cups)

2 large onions, sliced (about 2 cups)

1. Stir the soup, water, brown sugar, Worcestershire and thyme in a 3½-quart slow cooker. Add the pork chops and turn to coat with the soup mixture. Top with the apples and onions.

2. Cover and cook on LOW for 8 to 9 hours* or until the pork is cooked through.

*Or on HIGH for 4 to 5 hours

Campbell's Kitchen Tip: To make cleanup easier, spray the inside of your slow cooker crock with vegetable cooking spray before adding the food.

Creamy Chicken & Wild Rice

Makes: 8 servings
Prep: 10 minutes
Cook: 7 to 8 hours

2 cans (10¾ ounces **each**) Campbell's® Condensed Cream of Chicken Soup (Regular **or** 98% Fat Free)

1½ cups water

4 large carrots, thickly sliced (about 3 cups)

1 package (6 ounces) seasoned long-grain and wild rice mix

8 skinless, boneless chicken breast halves

1. Stir the soup, water, carrots, rice and seasoning packet in a 3½-quart slow cooker. Add the chicken and turn to coat with the soup mixture.

2. Cover and cook on LOW for 7 to 8 hours* or until the chicken is cooked through.

Or on HIGH for 4 to 5 hours

Serving Suggestion Tip: Serve with fresh broccoli steamed in Swanson® Chicken Broth for extra flavor.

Nacho Chicken & Rice Wraps

Makes: 10 servings
Prep: 5 minutes
Cook: 7 to 8 hours

2 cans (10¾ ounces **each**) Campbell's® Condensed Cheddar Cheese Soup

2 cups chunky salsa **or** picante sauce

1 cup water

1¼ cups **uncooked** regular long-grain white rice

2 pounds skinless, boneless chicken breasts, cut into cubes

10 flour tortillas (10-inch), warmed

1. Stir the soup, salsa, water, rice and chicken in a 3½-quart slow cooker.

2. Cover and cook on LOW for 7 to 8 hours* or until the chicken is cooked through.

3. Spoon about **1 cup** rice mixture down the center of each tortilla. Fold the tortilla around the filling.

Or on HIGH for 4 to 5 hours

Easy Substitution Tip: For firmer rice, substitute converted rice for the regular rice.

Melt-in-Your-Mouth Short Ribs

Makes: 6 servings
Prep: 10 minutes
Cook: 8 to 10 hours

3 pounds beef short ribs, cut into individual pieces

2 tablespoons packed brown sugar

3 cloves garlic, minced

1 teaspoon dried thyme leaves, crushed

¼ cup all-purpose flour

1 can (10½ ounces) Campbell's® Condensed French Onion Soup

1 bottle (12 fluid ounces) dark ale **or** beer

Hot mashed potatoes **or** buttered noodles

1. Put the ribs, brown sugar, garlic and thyme in a 3½- to 6-quart slow cooker. Sprinkle with the flour and toss to coat.

2. Stir the soup and ale in a small bowl. Pour the soup mixture over the ribs.

3. Cover and cook on LOW for 8 to 10 hours* or until the meat is fork-tender. Remove ribs from the cooker with a fork or kitchen tongs to a serving platter. Spoon off any fat from the sauce. Pour the sauce over the ribs. Serve with potatoes or noodles.

Or on HIGH for 4 to 5 hours

Southwestern Bean Medley

Makes: 8 servings
Prep: 10 minutes
Cook: 7 to 8 hours

1¾ cups Swanson® Vegetable Broth (Regular **or** Certified Organic)

1 tablespoon chili powder

1 teaspoon ground cumin

1 can (about 15 ounces) black beans, rinsed and drained

1 can (about 15 ounces) chickpeas (garbanzo beans), rinsed and drained

1 can (about 15 ounces) white kidney (cannellini) beans, rinsed and drained

½ cup dried lentils

1 can (14½ ounces) diced tomatoes and green chilies

Chopped fresh cilantro leaves

1. Stir the broth, chili powder, cumin, black beans, chickpeas, white kidney beans and lentils in a 3½-quart slow cooker.

2. Cover and cook on LOW for 6 to 7 hours*.

3. Add the tomatoes. Cover and cook for 1 hour more. Sprinkle with the cilantro.

Or on HIGH for 4 to 5 hours

Serving Suggestion Tip: For a complete meal, serve over hot cooked rice.

Creamy Chicken Tortilla Soup
Recipe on page 218

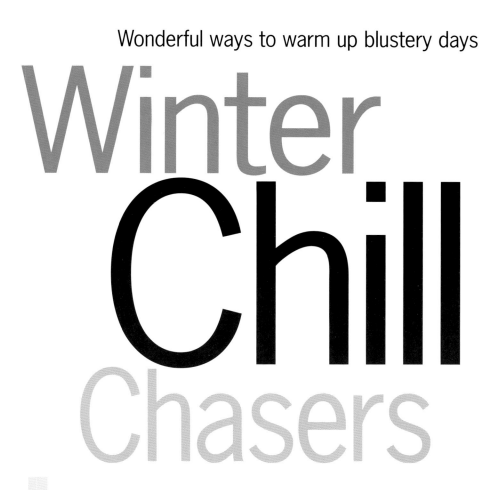

Winter Chill Chasers

Wonderful ways to warm up blustery days

It's only natural. When the thermometer drops, we want lots of homey, satisfying foods like soups and stews to lift our spirits and warm us up. Brimming with wholesome ingredients and the kind of delicious, mingled flavors that only come from long, slow simmering, they bring comfort by the bowlful.

These Campbell's® slow cooker recipes make it easy and convenient to fix hearty, meal-in-a-bowl main dishes, even if you have other things to do on a winter's day. They can simmer unsupervised in your kitchen for hours. Then, when it's time to eat, all you have to do is ladle out a big, steaming bowl for everyone, shut the door against the chill, and settle in. Ahhhh!

Creamy Chicken Tortilla Soup

(photo on page 216)

Makes: 6 servings
Prep: 15 minutes
Cook: 5 hours 15 minutes

1 cup chunky salsa

1 pound skinless, boneless chicken breasts, cut into ½-inch pieces

2 cups frozen whole kernel corn

1 can (about 15 ounces) black beans, rinsed and drained

2 cans (10¾ ounces **each**) Campbell's® Condensed Cream of Chicken Soup (Regular **or** 98% Fat Free)

1 soup can water

1 teaspoon ground cumin

4 corn tortillas (6-inch), cut into strips

1 cup shredded Cheddar cheese (4 ounces)

⅓ cup chopped fresh cilantro leaves

1. Stir the salsa, chicken, corn and beans in a 4-quart slow cooker.

2. Stir the soup, water and cumin in a small bowl. Pour over the chicken mixture.

3. Cover and cook on LOW for 5 hours*.

4. Stir the tortillas, cheese and cilantro into the cooker. Cover and cook for 15 minutes more. Serve with additional cheese, if desired.

Or on HIGH for 2 to 2½ hours

Beef & Vegetable Soup

Makes: 6 servings
Prep: 20 minutes
Cook: 8 to 10 hours 5 minutes

  1 pound beef for stew, cut into 1-inch pieces

     Ground black pepper

  2 tablespoons all-purpose flour

  2 tablespoons vegetable oil

  3 large onions, chopped (about 3 cups)

 12 small red potatoes, cut into quarters

  2 medium carrots, sliced (about 1 cup)

  4 cloves garlic, minced

  1 tablespoon chopped fresh thyme **or** 1 teaspoon dried thyme leaves, crushed

  4 cups Swanson® Beef Broth (Regular, Lower Sodium **or** Certified Organic)

  2 tablespoons tomato paste

  1½ teaspoons instant coffee powder **or** granules

     Sour cream (optional)

     Chopped green onions (optional)

1. Sprinkle the beef with black pepper and coat with the flour. Heat the oil in a 10-inch skillet over medium-high heat. Add the beef and cook until it's well browned, stirring often.

2. Place the onions, potatoes, carrots, garlic and thyme in a 3½-quart slow cooker. Top with the beef. Stir **1 cup** of the broth, tomato paste and coffee in a small bowl. Pour the coffee mixture and remaining broth into the cooker.

3. Cover and cook on LOW for 8 to 10 hours* or until the meat is fork-tender. Serve with sour cream and green onions, if desired.

Or on HIGH for 4 to 5 hours

Barley and Lentil Soup

Makes: 8 servings
Prep: 10 minutes
Cook: 8 to 9 hours

8 cups Swanson® Beef Broth (Regular, Lower Sodium **or** Certified Organic)

2 cloves garlic, minced

1 teaspoon dried oregano leaves, crushed

4 large carrots, sliced (about 3 cups)

1 large onion, chopped (about 1 cup)

½ cup dried lentils

½ cup **uncooked** barley

1. Stir the broth, garlic, oregano, carrots, onion, lentils and barley in a 3½- to 6-quart slow cooker.

2. Cover and cook on LOW for 8 to 9 hours* or until the beans and barley are tender.

*Or on HIGH for 4 to 5 hours

Hearty Beef Stew

Makes: 6 servings
Prep: 10 minutes
Cook: 10 to 12 hours 15 minutes

1½ pounds beef for stew, cut into 1-inch pieces

Ground black pepper

¼ cup all-purpose flour

1 tablespoon vegetable oil

2½ cups cubed potatoes

4 medium carrots, sliced (about 2 cups)

2 medium onions, cut into wedges

4 cloves garlic, minced

3¼ cups Swanson® Beef Broth (Regular, Lower Sodium **or** Certified Organic)

1 tablespoon Worcestershire sauce

1 teaspoon dried thyme leaves, crushed

1 bay leaf

1 cup frozen peas

1. Sprinkle the beef with black pepper and coat with **2 tablespoons** of the flour. Heat the oil in a 12-inch skillet over medium-high heat. Add the beef in 2 batches and cook until it's well browned, stirring often.

2. Place the potatoes, carrots, onions and garlic into a 5-quart slow cooker. Top with the beef. Add **3 cups** of the broth, Worcestershire, thyme and bay leaf.

3. Cover and cook on LOW for 10 to 12 hours* or until the meat is fork-tender. Remove the bay leaf.

4. Stir the remaining broth into the remaining flour in a small bowl. Stir the flour mixture and peas into the cooker. Turn the heat to HIGH. Cover and cook 15 minutes or until slightly thickened.

Or cook on HIGH for 5 to 6 hours

Southwestern Chicken & White Bean Soup

Makes: 6 servings
Prep: 15 minutes
Cook: 8 to 10 hours

1 tablespoon vegetable oil

1 pound skinless, boneless chicken breasts, cut into 1-inch pieces

1¾ cups Swanson® Chicken Broth (Regular, Natural Goodness™ **or** Certified Organic)

1 cup chunky salsa

3 cloves garlic, minced

2 teaspoons ground cumin

1 can (about 15 ounces) small white beans, rinsed and drained

1 cup frozen whole kernel corn

1 large onion, chopped (about 1 cup)

1. Heat the oil in a 10-inch skillet over medium-high heat. Add the chicken and cook until it's well browned, stirring often.

2. Stir the broth, salsa, garlic, cumin, beans, corn and onion in a 3½-quart slow cooker. Add the chicken.

3. Cover and cook on LOW for 8 to 10 hours* or until the chicken is cooked through.

*Or on HIGH for 4 to 5 hours

Veal Stew with Garden Vegetables

Makes: 6 servings
Prep: 10 minutes
Cook: 8 to 10 hours 10 minutes

2 to 2½ pounds veal for stew, cut into 1-inch pieces

Ground black pepper

2 tablespoons olive oil

1 bag (16 ounces) fresh **or** frozen whole baby carrots (about 2½ cups)

1 large onion, diced (about 1 cup)

4 cloves garlic, minced

¼ cup all-purpose flour

2 cups Swanson® Chicken Broth (Regular, Natural Goodness™ **or** Certified Organic)

½ teaspoon dried rosemary leaves, crushed

1 can (14½ ounces) diced tomatoes

1 cup frozen peas

Hot cooked rice **or** barley

1. Season the veal with the black pepper.

2. Heat the oil in a 6-quart saucepot. Add the veal in 2 batches and cook until it's well browned, stirring often. Remove the veal with a slotted spoon and put it in a 3½- to 6-quart slow cooker.

3. Add the carrots, onion and garlic. Sprinkle with the flour and toss to coat. Stir the broth, rosemary and tomatoes into the cooker.

4. Cover and cook on LOW for 7 to 8 hours*.

5. Stir the peas into the cooker. Cover and cook for 1 hour more or until the meat is fork-tender. Serve over the rice or barley.

Or on HIGH for 4 to 5 hours

Easy Substitution Tip: Substitute skinless, boneless chicken thighs, cut into 1-inch pieces for the veal.

Slow-Simmered Chicken Rice Soup

Makes: 8 servings
Prep: 15 minutes
Cook: 7 to 8 hours

½ cup **uncooked** wild rice

½ cup **uncooked** regular long-grain white rice

1 tablespoon vegetable oil

5¼ cups Swanson® Chicken Broth (Regular, Natural Goodness™ **or** Certified Organic)

2 teaspoons dried thyme leaves, crushed

¼ teaspoon crushed red pepper

2 stalks celery, coarsely chopped (about 1 cup)

1 medium onion, chopped (about ½ cup)

1 pound skinless, boneless chicken breasts, cut into cubes

Sour cream (optional)

Chopped green onions (optional)

1. Stir the wild rice, white rice and oil in a 3½-quart slow cooker. Cover and cook on HIGH for 15 minutes.

2. Stir the broth, thyme, red pepper, celery, onion and chicken into the cooker. Turn the heat to LOW. Cover and cook on LOW for 7 to 8 hours* or until the chicken is cooked through.

3. Serve with the sour cream and green onions, if desired.

Or on HIGH for 4 to 5 hours

Time-Saving Tip: Speed preparation by substituting 3 cans (4.5 ounces **each**) Swanson® Premium Chunk Chicken Breast, drained, for the raw chicken.

White Bean with Fennel Soup

Makes: 6 servings
Prep: 15 minutes
Cook: 7 to 8 hours

4 cups Swanson® Vegetable Broth (Regular **or** Certified Organic)

⅛ teaspoon ground black pepper

1 small bulb fennel (about ½ pound), trimmed and sliced (about 2 cups)

1 medium onion, chopped (about ½ cup)

2 cloves garlic, minced

1 package (10 ounces) frozen leaf spinach

1 can (14½ ounces) diced tomatoes

1 can (about 15 ounces) white kidney (cannellini) beans, undrained

1. Stir the broth, black pepper, fennel, onion and garlic in a 5½- to 6-quart slow cooker.

2. Cover and cook on LOW for 6 to 7 hours.

3. Add the spinach, tomatoes and undrained beans. Turn the heat to HIGH. Cover and cook for 1 hour more or until the vegetables are tender.

Hearty Pork Stew

Makes: 8 servings
Prep: 25 minutes
Cook: 7 to 8 hours

2   pounds sweet potatoes, peeled and cut into 2-inch pieces
    (about 2 cups)

    2-pound boneless pork shoulder roast, cut into 1-inch pieces

1   can (14½ ounces) Campbell's® Chicken Gravy

1   teaspoon dried thyme leaves, crushed

½   teaspoon crushed red pepper

1   can (15 ounces) black-eyed peas, rinsed and drained

1. Put the potatoes in a 4- to 6-quart slow cooker. Top with the pork.

2. Stir the gravy, thyme, red pepper and peas in a small bowl. Pour over the pork and potatoes.

3. Cover and cook on LOW for 7 to 8 hours* or until the meat is fork-tender.

Or on HIGH for 4 to 5 hours

Leftover Tip: Freeze leftovers of this hearty stew as individual portions. Just reheat in a microwave for fast weeknight dinners!

Slow-Cooker Beef & Mushroom Stew

Makes: 6 servings
Prep: 10 minutes
Cook: 10 to 12 hours 25 minutes

1½ pounds boneless beef bottom round **or** chuck roast, cut into 1-inch pieces

Ground black pepper

¼ cup all-purpose flour

2 tablespoons vegetable oil

1 can (10½ ounces) Campbell's® Condensed French Onion Soup

1 cup Burgundy **or** other dry red wine

2 cloves garlic, minced

1 teaspoon dried Italian seasoning, crushed

1 package (10 ounces) mushrooms cut in half (about 3 cups)

3 medium carrots, cut into 2-inch pieces (about 1½ cups)

1 cup frozen small whole white onions

¼ cup water

1. Sprinkle the beef with black pepper and coat with **2 tablespoons** of the flour. Heat the oil in a 12-inch skillet over medium-high heat. Add the beef in 2 batches and cook until it's well browned, stirring often. Remove the beef with a slotted spoon and put in a 3½-quart slow cooker.

2. Stir the soup, wine, garlic, Italian seasoning, mushrooms, carrots and onions into the cooker.

3. Cover and cook on LOW for 10 to 12 hours* or until the meat is fork-tender.

4. Stir the water into the remaining flour in a small bowl. Stir the flour mixture into the cooker. Turn the heat to HIGH. Cover and cook for 15 minutes or until slightly thickened.

*Or on HIGH for 4 to 5 hours

Hearty Mixed Bean Stew with Sausage

Makes: 8 servings
Prep: 10 minutes
Cook: 8 to 9 hours 5 minutes

¾ pound sweet Italian pork sausage, casing removed

10 cups Swanson® Chicken Broth (Regular, Natural Goodness™
      or Certified Organic)

¼ teaspoon ground black pepper

2 medium carrots, chopped (about ⅔ cup)

1 stalk celery, chopped (about ½ cup)

¾ cup **each** dried pinto, navy **and** kidney beans

6 sun-dried tomatoes in oil, drained and thinly sliced
      (about ¼ cup)

   Grated Parmesan cheese

1. Cook the sausage in a 10-inch skillet over medium-high heat until it's well browned, stirring frequently to break up meat. Remove the sausage with a slotted spoon and put in a 5- to 5½-quart slow cooker.

2. Stir the broth, black pepper, carrots, celery and pinto, navy and kidney beans into the cooker.

3. Cover and cook on LOW for 7 or 8 hours*.

4. Stir in the tomatoes. Cover and cook for 1 hour more or until the beans are tender. Serve with the cheese.

Or on HIGH for 4 to 4½ hours

Chipotle Chili

Makes: 8 servings
Prep: 15 minutes
Cook: 8 to 9 hours

1 jar (16 ounces) Pace® Chipotle **or** Regular Chunky Salsa

1 cup water

2 tablespoons chili powder

1 large onion, chopped (about 1 cup)

2 pounds beef for stew, cut into ½-inch pieces

1 can (about 19 ounces) red kidney beans, rinsed and drained

Shredded Cheddar cheese (optional)

Sour cream (optional)

1. Stir the salsa, water, chili powder, onion, beef and beans in a 3½-quart slow cooker.

2. Cover and cook on LOW for 8 to 9 hours* or until the meat is fork-tender. Serve with the cheese and sour cream, if desired.

Or on HIGH for 4 to 5 hours

Serving Suggestion Tip: Serve with savory corn muffins made from your favorite corn muffin mix and Swanson® Chicken or Seasoned Broth. Follow the package directions, substituting an equal amount of broth for the milk.

Greek-Style Beef Stew

Makes: 6 servings
Prep: 10 minutes
Cook: 8 to 10 hours

2 to 2½ pounds boneless beef bottom round **or** chuck pot roast, cut into 1-inch pieces

1 bag (16 ounces) frozen small white onions (about 4 cups)

1 bag (16 ounces) fresh **or** frozen whole baby carrots (about 2½ cups)

2 tablespoons all-purpose flour

1¾ cups Swanson® Beef Broth (Regular, Lower Sodium **or** Certified Organic)

1 can (5.5 fluid ounces) V8® Vegetable Juice

1 tablespoon packed brown sugar

Bouquet Garni

Hot buttered noodles

1. Place the beef, onions and carrots in a 3½- to 6-quart slow cooker. Sprinkle with the flour and toss to coat.

2. Stir the broth, vegetable juice and brown sugar in a small bowl. Pour over the beef and vegetables. Submerge the *Bouquet Garni* into the broth mixture.

3. Cover and cook on LOW for 8 to 10 hours* or until the meat is fork-tender. Remove the *Bouquet Garni*. Serve over the noodles.

Or on HIGH 4 to 5 hours

Bouquet Garni: Lay a **4-inch square of cheesecloth** flat on counter. Place ½ **teaspoon** whole cloves, **1** cinnamon stick and **1** bay leaf in the center of the cloth. Bring the corners of cheesecloth together and tie with kitchen string into a bundle.

Not Your Gramma's Kugel
Recipe on page 242

Classic favorites made simple

Heritage Recipes

Slow cooking is the perfect method for preparing many of the traditional, home-style dishes we all grew up with. What makes it so ideal? Sheer ease and convenience. Today's slow cookers skip the lengthy stovetop simmering, laborious stirring, and constant attention required in the past. Yet they faithfully reproduce the same wonderful results: fork-tender meats and poultry, succulent vegetables and concentrated sauces brimming with flavor.

Slow cookers also do an excellent job of re-creating scrumptious desserts like gramma used to make—from dense bread pudding to moist spice cake. So celebrate our food heritage with these familiar recipes and discover just how easy it is to make tasty classics the slow cooker way.

Not Your Gramma's Kugel

(photo on page 240)

Makes: 6 servings
Prep: 10 minutes
Cook: 2 to 2½ hours 5 minutes

Vegetable cooking spray

1 package (12 ounces) medium egg noodles

½ cup currants

1 can (10¾ ounces) Campbell's® Condensed Cheddar Cheese Soup

1 cup small curd cottage cheese

¾ cup sugar

1 teaspoon grated orange peel

2 eggs

1. Spray the inside of a 3½-quart slow cooker with cooking spray.

2. Cook the noodles according to the package directions until almost done. Drain in a colander and place in the cooker. Sprinkle with the currants.

3. Beat the soup, cottage cheese, sugar, orange peel and eggs in a small bowl. Pour over the noodles. Stir to coat.

4. Cover and cook on LOW for 2 to 2½ hours or until set. Serve warm.

Leftover Tip: For a tasty breakfast, reheat leftover kugel in the microwave.

Spiced Pot Roast

Makes: 8 servings
Prep: 15 minutes
Cook: 8 to 9 hours
Stand: 10 minutes

   4-pound boneless beef bottom round **or** chuck pot roast

4 cloves garlic

1 tablespoon chili powder

½ teaspoon ground coriander

½ teaspoon ground cumin

2 cans (10½ ounces **each**) Campbell's® Condensed Beef Broth

2 large onions, sliced (about 2 cups)

1 can (about 15 ounces) whole tomatoes

1 can (about 15 ounces) red kidney beans, rinsed and drained

¾ cup **uncooked** regular long-grain white rice

1. Cut 4 evenly-spaced slits in the roast. Insert the garlic cloves into each slit. Mix the chili powder, coriander and cumin in a cup. Rub over the roast. Place the roast in a 6-quart slow cooker.

2. Stir the broth, onion, tomatoes, beans and rice in a medium bowl. Pour over the roast. Cover and cook on LOW for 8 to 9 hours* or until the meat is fork-tender.

3. Remove the roast from the cooker to a cutting board and let it stand for 10 minutes before slicing. Thinly slice the roast and put on a serving platter. Pour the juices from the cooker into a gravy boat and serve with the roast.

Or on HIGH for 4 to 5 hours

Herbed Turkey Breast

Makes: 8 servings
Prep: 10 minutes
Cook: 8 to 9 hours
Stand: 10 minutes

1 can (10¾ ounces) Campbell's® Condensed Cream of Mushroom Soup (Regular **or** 98% Fat Free)

½ cup water

4½- to 5-pound turkey breast*

1 teaspoon poultry seasoning

1 tablespoon chopped fresh parsley

Hot mashed potatoes

1. Stir the soup and water in a 3½- to 6-quart slow cooker. Rinse the turkey with cold water and pat dry. Rub the turkey with the poultry seasoning and place in the cooker. Sprinkle with the parsley.

2. Cover and cook on LOW for 8 to 9 hours**.

3. Remove the turkey from the cooker to a cutting board and let it stand for 10 minutes before slicing. Thinly slice the turkey and put on a serving platter. Pour the juices from the cooker into a gravy boat and serve with the turkey. Serve with the mashed potatoes.

If using a frozen turkey breast, thaw it before cooking.

**Or on HIGH for 4 to 5 hours*

Apricot Glazed Pork Roast

Makes: 8 servings
Prep: 5 minutes
Cook: 8 to 9 hours
Stand: 10 minutes

1 can (10½ ounces) Campbell's® Condensed Chicken Broth

1 jar (18 ounces) apricot preserves

2 tablespoons Dijon-style mustard

1 large onion, chopped (about 1 cup)

3½- to 4-pound boneless pork loin

1. Stir the broth, preserves, mustard and onion in a 3½-quart slow cooker. Cut the pork to fit. Add the pork to the cooker and turn to coat with the broth mixture.

2. Cover and cook on LOW for 8 to 9 hours* or until the meat is fork-tender.

3. Remove the pork from the cooker to a cutting board and let it stand for 10 minutes before slicing. Thinly slice the pork and put on a serving platter. Pour the juices from the cooker into a gravy boat and serve with the pork.

Or on HIGH for 4 to 5 hours

For a thicker sauce, stir **2 tablespoons** cornstarch and **2 tablespoons** water in a small cup. Remove the roast from the cooker. Stir the cornstarch mixture into cooker. Turn heat to HIGH. Cover and cook for 10 minutes or until the mixture boils and thickens.

Serving Suggestion Tip: Use some of the glaze from the roast for a delicious mashed potato topping.

Slow-Cooked Autumn Brisket

Makes: 8 servings
Prep: 20 minutes
Cook: 8 to 9 hours
Stand: 10 minutes

   3-pound boneless beef brisket

1   small head cabbage (about 1 pound), cut into 8 wedges

1   large sweet potato (about ¾ pound), peeled and cut into
      1-inch pieces

1   large onion, cut into 8 wedges

1   medium Granny Smith apple, cored and cut into 8 wedges

2   cans (10¾ ounces **each**) Campbell's® Condensed Cream of
      Celery Soup (Regular **or** 98% Fat Free)

1   cup water

2   teaspoons caraway seed (optional)

1. Season the brisket, if desired.

2. Put the brisket in a 6-quart slow cooker. Top with the cabbage,
sweet potato, onion and apple.

3. Stir the soup, water and caraway, if desired, in a medium bowl.
Pour the soup mixture over the brisket and vegetable mixture.

4. Cover and cook on LOW for 8 to 9 hours* or until the meat is
fork-tender.

5. Remove the brisket from the cooker to a cutting board and let it
stand for 10 minutes before slicing. Thinly slice brisket across the
grain and put on a serving platter. Remove the vegetables and fruit
with a slotted spoon and put on platter. Pour the juices from the
cooker into a gravy boat and serve with the brisket.

Or on HIGH for 4 to 5 hours

Campbell's Kitchen Tip: Try to buy roasts and other large cuts of meat
that fit into your slow cooker, or plan on trimming them to fit.

Slow Cooker Chicken & Dumplings

Makes: 8 servings
Prep: 20 minutes
Cook: 7 to 8 hours 30 minutes

2   medium Yukon Gold potatoes, cut into 1-inch pieces
(about 2 cups)

2   cups fresh **or** frozen whole baby carrots

2   stalks celery, sliced (about 1 cup)

3   skinless, boneless chicken breasts, cut into 1-inch pieces

2   cans (10¾ ounces **each**) Campbell's® Condensed Cream
of Chicken Soup (Regular **or** 98% Fat Free)

1   cup water

1   teaspoon dried thyme leaves, crushed

¼   teaspoon ground black pepper

2   cups all-purpose baking mix

⅔   cup milk

1. Put the potatoes, carrots, celery and chicken in a 6-quart slow cooker.

2. Stir the soup, water, thyme and black pepper in a small bowl. Pour over the chicken and vegetables.

3. Cover and cook on LOW for 7 to 8 hours* or until the chicken is cooked through.

4. Stir the baking mix and milk in a small bowl until the ingredients are mixed. Drop the batter by spoonfuls over the chicken mixture. Turn the heat to HIGH. Tilt the lid to vent and cook for 30 minutes more or until the dumplings are cooked in the center.

Or on HIGH for 4 to 5 hours

Campbell's Kitchen Tip: Leaving the lid slightly ajar while cooking the dumplings prevents condensation from dripping onto the food.

Ham & Scalloped Potato Casserole

Makes: 8 servings
Prep: 25 minutes
Cook: 7 to 8 hours

Vegetable cooking spray

4 pounds potatoes, peeled and thinly sliced (about 8 cups)

1 pound diced cooked ham (2 cups)

1 large onion, sliced (about 1 cup)

2 cans (10¾ ounces **each**) Campbell's® Condensed Cheddar Cheese Soup

1 cup milk

1 teaspoon paprika

1. Spray the inside of a 5- to 6-quart slow cooker with cooking spray.

2. Layer the potatoes, ham and onion in the cooker.

3. Stir the soup and milk in a medium bowl. Pour over the potato mixture. Sprinkle with the paprika.

4. Cover and cook on LOW for 7 to 8 hours*.

Or on HIGH for 4 to 5 hours

Serving Suggestion Tip: Serve this classic country casserole with applesauce and a tossed salad.

Country-Style Ribs

Makes: 8 servings
Prep: 10 minutes
Cook: 7 to 8 hours 10 minutes

4   pounds pork country-style ribs, cut into serving pieces

Ground black pepper

3   cloves garlic, minced

1   can (10¾ ounces) Campbell's® Condensed Tomato Soup (Regular **or** Healthy Request®)

2   tablespoons packed brown sugar

2   tablespoons cider vinegar

1   tablespoon Worcestershire sauce

2   teaspoons dry mustard

1. Sprinkle the ribs with black pepper.

2. Cook the ribs in 2 batches in a 12-inch skillet over medium-high heat until they're well browned on all sides. Place the ribs in a 5- to 6-quart slow cooker and sprinkle with garlic.

3. Stir the soup, brown sugar, vinegar, Worcestershire and mustard in a small bowl. Pour over the ribs and toss to coat.

4. Cover and cook on LOW for 7 to 8 hours* or until the meat is fork-tender. Remove the ribs from the cooker with a fork or tongs to a serving platter. Pour the sauce from the cooker over the ribs.

Or on HIGH for 4 to 5 hours

Time-Saving Tip: Ribs can also be cooked without the browning step. Spoon off the fat from the sauce before serving.

Chocolate Almond Bread Pudding

Makes: 6 servings
Prep: 10 minutes
Cook: 2½ to 3 hours

Vegetable cooking spray

10 slices Pepperidge Farm® White Sandwich Bread, cut into cubes (about 5 cups)

½ cup dried cherries, chopped

½ cup semi-sweet chocolate pieces

1¾ cups milk

½ cup sugar

⅓ cup unsweetened baking cocoa

½ teaspoon almond **or** vanilla extract

4 eggs

Sweetened whipped cream (optional)

Toasted almonds (optional)

1. Spray the inside of a 4½- to 5-quart slow cooker with cooking spray.

2. Place the bread in the cooker. Sprinkle with the cherries and chocolate.

3. Beat the milk, sugar, cocoa, almond extract and eggs in a medium bowl. Pour over the bread mixture. Stir and push the bread cubes into the milk mixture to coat.

4. Cover and cook on LOW for 2½ to 3 hours or until set. Serve warm with whipped cream and almonds, if desired.

Raisin Cinnamon Bread Pudding

Makes: 6 servings
Prep: 10 minutes
Cook: 2½ to 3 hours

Vegetable cooking spray

10 slices Pepperidge Farm® Raisin Cinnamon Swirl Bread, cut into cubes (about 5 cups)

1 can (14 ounces) sweetened condensed milk

1 cup water

1 teaspoon vanilla extract

4 eggs

Ice cream (optional)

1. Spray the inside of a 4½- to 5-quart slow cooker with cooking spray.

2. Place the bread in the cooker.

3. Beat the milk, water, vanilla and eggs in a medium bowl. Pour over the bread mixture. Stir and push the bread cubes into the milk mixture to coat.

4. Cover and cook on LOW for 2½ to 3 hours or until set. Serve warm with ice cream, if desired.

Campbell's Kitchen Tip: Even when it's too hot to bake, you can surprise your family with fresh, homemade desserts made in the slow cooker.

Brown Sugar Spice Cake

Makes: 8 servings
Prep: 10 minutes
Cook: 2 to 2½ hours

Vegetable cooking spray

1 can (10¾ ounces) Campbell's® Condensed Tomato Soup (Regular **or** Healthy Request®)

½ cup water

2 eggs

1 box (about 18 ounces) spice cake mix

1¼ cups hot water

¾ cup packed brown sugar

1 teaspoon ground cinnamon

Vanilla ice cream

1. Spray the inside of a 3½- to 4-quart slow cooker with cooking spray.

2. Beat the soup, water, eggs and cake mix according to the package directions. Pour into the cooker.

3. Stir the water, brown sugar and cinnamon in a small bowl. Pour over the batter.

4. Cover and cook on HIGH for 2 to 2½ hours or until a toothpick inserted in the center comes out clean.

5. Spoon the cake into bowls, scooping sauce from bottom of cooker. Serve warm with ice cream.

Campbell's Kitchen Tip: This is a great dessert to make when you're entertaining and the oven is occupied with another dish.

Beef Bourguignonne
Recipe on page 262

Slow cooking with an international flair

A World of Flavors

Slow cooking is more than just a convenient way to prepare familiar comfort foods and family favorites. If you enjoy trying foods from other countries or experimenting with regional flavors, the slow cooker is a perfect travel partner!

Whether you have a yen for Asian or crave some Cajun spice, your slow cooker can prepare just about any type of meal you can imagine and deliver authentic-tasting results. This collection of international recipes features the predominant flavors of several of today's most popular ethnic and regional cuisines. By preparing these dishes in your slow cooker, you'll make it easy as well as fun for your family to get adventurous.

Beef Bourguignonne

(photo on page 260)

Makes: 6 servings
Prep: 10 minutes
Cook: 8 to 9 hours

1 can (10¾ ounces) Campbell's® Condensed Golden Mushroom Soup

1 cup Burgundy **or** other dry red wine

2 cloves garlic, minced

1 teaspoon dried thyme leaves, crushed

6 ounces small button mushrooms (about 2 cups)

2 cups fresh **or** frozen whole baby carrots

1 cup frozen small whole onions

1½ pounds boneless beef top round steak, 1½ inches thick, cut into 1-inch pieces

1. Stir the soup, wine, garlic, thyme, mushrooms, carrots, onions and beef in a 3½-quart slow cooker.

2. Cover and cook on LOW for 8 to 9 hours* or until the meat is fork-tender.

Or on HIGH for 4 to 5 hours

Campbell's Kitchen Tip: Slow cookers work best half full to three-quarters full, so go ahead and fill it up. Freeze the leftovers for another meal.

Slow Cooker Swiss Steak

Makes: 6 servings
Prep: 10 minutes
Cook: 8 to 10 hours 10 minutes

- 1 tablespoon vegetable oil
- 1½ pounds boneless beef round steak, cut into 6 pieces
- 6 to 8 new potatoes (about ½ pound), cut into quarters
- 1½ cups fresh **or** frozen whole baby carrots
- 1 medium onion, sliced (about ½ cup)
- 1 can (14½ ounces) diced tomatoes with basil, garlic and oregano
- 1 can (10¼ ounces) Campbell's® Beef Gravy

1. Heat the oil in a 12-inch skillet over medium-high heat. Add the beef in 2 batches and cook until it's well browned, stirring often. Remove the beef with a slotted spoon and put in a 3½-quart slow cooker.

2. Place the potatoes, carrots and onion into the cooker. Stir the tomatoes and gravy in a small bowl. Pour over the beef and vegetables.

3. Cover and cook on LOW for 8 to 10 hours* or until the meat is fork-tender.

*Or on HIGH for 4 to 5 hours

Campbell's Kitchen Tip: Slow cooking actually tenderizes less-expensive cuts of meat like round steak, so you save time, effort and money.

Creamy Blush Sauce with Turkey & Penne

Makes: 8 servings
Prep: 10 minutes
Cook: 7 to 8 hours

4 turkey thighs, skin removed (about 3 pounds)

1 jar (1 pound 9.75 ounces) Prego® Chunky Mushrooms & Green Pepper Italian Sauce

½ teaspoon crushed red pepper

½ cup half-and-half

Tube-shaped pasta (penne), cooked and drained

Grated Parmesan cheese

1. Put the turkey in a 3½- to 5-quart slow cooker. Pour the Italian sauce over the turkey and sprinkle with the red pepper.

2. Cover and cook on LOW for 7 to 8 hours* or until the turkey is fork-tender and cooked through. Remove the turkey from the cooker with a fork or tongs to a cutting board. Remove the turkey meat from the bones.

3. Stir the turkey meat and the half-and-half into the cooker. Cover and cook for 10 minutes or until hot. Spoon the sauce over the turkey and pasta. Sprinkle with the cheese.

Or on HIGH for 4 to 5 hours

Easy Substitution Tip: Substitute 8 bone-in chicken thighs (about 2 pounds) for the turkey thighs. Makes 4 servings.

Coq au Vin

Makes: 6 servings
Prep: 10 minutes
Cook: 8 to 10 hours

1 package (10 ounces) sliced mushrooms (about 4 cups)

1 bag (16 ounces) frozen small white onions (about 4 cups)

1 sprig fresh rosemary

2 to 2½ pounds skinless, boneless chicken (combination of thighs and breasts), cut into 1-inch strips

¼ cup cornstarch

1 can (10¾ ounces) Campbell's® Condensed Golden Mushroom Soup

1 cup Burgundy **or** other dry red wine

Hot mashed **or** oven-roasted potatoes

1. Put the mushrooms, onions, rosemary and chicken in a 3½-quart slow cooker.

2. Stir the cornstarch, soup and wine in a small bowl. Pour the soup mixture over the chicken and vegetables.

3. Cover and cook on LOW for 8 to 10 hours*. Remove rosemary sprig. Serve with potatoes.

Or on HIGH for 4 to 5 hours

Jambalaya

Makes: 6 servings
Prep: 15 minutes
Cook: 7 to 8 hours 40 minutes

2 cups Swanson® Chicken Broth (Regular, Natural Goodness™ **or** Certified Organic)

1 tablespoon Creole seasoning

1 large green pepper, diced (about 1⅓ cups)

1 large onion, diced (about 1 cup)

2 large celery stalks, diced (about 1 cup)

1 can (about 14½ ounces) diced tomatoes

1 pound kielbasa, cut into cubes

¾ pound skinless, boneless chicken thighs, cut into cubes

1 cup **uncooked** regular long-grain white rice

½ pound fresh medium shrimp, shelled and deveined

1. Stir the broth, Creole seasoning, pepper, onion, celery, tomatoes, kielbasa, chicken and rice in a 3½- to 6-quart slow cooker.

2. Cover and cook on LOW for 7 to 8 hours*.

3. Stir the shrimp into the cooker. Cover and cook for 40 minutes more or until done.

Or on HIGH for 4 to 5 hours

Beef Taco Casserole

Makes: 8 servings
Prep: 10 minutes
Cook Time: 7 to 8 hours 10 minutes

2   pounds ground beef

1   can (10¾ ounces) Campbell's® Condensed Tomato Soup (Regular **or** Healthy Request®)

½   cup water

1   can (14½ ounces) diced tomatoes with green chilies

8   corn tortillas (6-inch), cut into ½-inch strips

1   cup shredded Cheddar cheese (4 ounces)

3   green onions, chopped (about ⅓ cup)

    Sour cream

1. Cook beef in 2 batches in large skillet over medium-high heat, stirring to separate meat. Pour off fat.

2. Mix beef, soup, water, tomatoes and tortillas in 3½- to 5-quart slow cooker.

3. Cover and cook on LOW for 7 to 8 hours*. Stir in cheese. Cover and cook 5 minutes. Sprinkle with green onions and serve with sour cream.

Or on HIGH 4 to 5 hours

Ratatouille with Penne

Makes: 4 servings
Prep: 15 minutes
Cook: 5½ to 6 hours

1 can (10¾ ounces) Campbell's® Condensed Tomato Soup (Regular **or** Healthy Request®)

1 tablespoon olive oil

⅛ teaspoon ground black pepper

1 small eggplant, peeled and cut into ½-inch cubes (about 5 cups)

1 medium zucchini, thinly sliced (about 1½ cups)

1 medium red pepper, diced (about 1 cup)

1 large onion, sliced (about 1 cup)

1 clove garlic, minced

Tube-shaped pasta (penne), cooked and drained

Grated Parmesan cheese

1. Stir the soup, olive oil, black pepper, eggplant, zucchini, red pepper, onion and garlic in a 4- to 5½-quart slow cooker.

2. Cover and cook on LOW for 5½ to 6 hours* or until the vegetables are tender.

3. Serve over the pasta with the cheese.

Or on HIGH for 2½ to 3 hours

Serving Suggestion Tip: Serve with Pepperidge Farm® Hot & Crusty Italian Bread.

Mexican Black Bean & Beef Soup

Makes: 8 servings
Prep: 10 minutes
Cook: 8 to 9 hours

2 cups water

1 jar (16 ounces) Pace® Chunky Salsa, any variety

1 tablespoon chopped fresh cilantro leaves

1 teaspoon ground cumin

1 large onion, chopped (about 1 cup)

1 cup frozen whole kernel corn

1 can (about 15 ounces) black beans, rinsed and drained

1 pound beef for stew, cut into ½-inch pieces

1. Stir the water, salsa, cilantro, cumin, onion, corn, beans and beef in a 3½- to 6-quart slow cooker.

2. Cover and cook on LOW 8 to 9 hours* or until the meat is fork-tender.

Or on HIGH 4 to 5 hours

Serving Suggestion Tip: Serve with a mixed green salad and warm flour **or** corn tortillas.

Chicken Cacciatore

Makes: 6 servings
Prep: 10 minutes
Cook: 7 to 8 hours 10 minutes

1¾ cups Swanson® Chicken Broth (Regular, Natural Goodness™ **or** Certified Organic)

1 teaspoon garlic powder

2 cans (14½ ounces **each**) diced Italian-style tomatoes

4 cups mushrooms, cut in half (about 12 ounces)

2 large onions, chopped (about 2 cups)

3 pounds chicken parts, skin removed

   Hot cooked spaghetti

1. Stir the broth, garlic powder, tomatoes, mushrooms and onions in a 3½-quart slow cooker. Add the chicken and turn to coat with the broth mixture.

2. Cover and cook on LOW for 7 to 8 hours* or until the chicken is cooked through. Serve over the spaghetti.

Or on HIGH for 4 to 5 hours

For thicker sauce, stir **2 tablespoons** cornstarch and **2 tablespoons** water in a small cup. Remove the chicken from the cooker. Stir the cornstarch mixture into the cooker. Turn heat to HIGH. Cover and cook for 10 minutes or until the mixture boils and thickens.

Easy Substitution Tip: Make Simple Seasoned Pasta instead of spaghetti. Bring 3½ cups of Swanson® Chicken Broth with Roasted Garlic to a boil. Stir in 3 cups **uncooked** corkscrew-shaped pasta (rotini). Simmer gently over medium heat for 10 minutes or until the pasta is tender but still firm and the mixture is saucy.

Chicken & Rice Pacifica

Makes: 8 servings
Prep: 20 minutes
Cook: 7 to 8 hours

2 cans (10½ ounces **each**) Campbell's® Condensed Chicken Broth

1 cup water

¼ cup soy sauce

2 cloves garlic, minced

8 skinless, boneless chicken thighs (about 2 pounds), cut into 1½-inch pieces

1 medium green **or** red pepper, cut into 1½-inch pieces (about 1 cup)

4 medium green onions, cut into 2-inch pieces (about 1 cup)

1 can (20 ounces) pineapple chunks in juice, undrained

1 cup **uncooked** regular long-grain white rice

Toasted sliced almonds

1. Stir the broth, water, soy sauce, garlic, chicken, pepper, onions, pineapple with juice and rice in a 6-quart slow cooker.

2. Cover and cook on LOW for 7 to 8 hours* or until chicken is no longer pink.

3. Sprinkle with the almonds before serving.

Or on HIGH for 4 to 5 hours

Campbell's Kitchen Tip: To toast almonds, arrange almonds in single layer in a shallow baking pan. Bake at 350°F. for 10 minutes or until lightly browned.

Zesty Slow Cooker Italian Pot Roast

Makes: 5 servings
Prep: 45 minutes
Cook: 10 to 12 hours
Stand: 10 minutes

	2½-pound boneless beef bottom round **or** chuck pot roast
½	teaspoon ground black pepper
4	medium potatoes, (about 1 pound), cut into quarters
2	cups fresh **or** frozen baby carrots
1	stalk celery, cut into 1-inch pieces
1	medium plum tomato, diced
1	can (10¾ ounces) Campbell's® Condensed Tomato Soup (Regular **or** Healthy Request®)
½	cup water
1	tablespoon chopped roasted garlic* **or** fresh garlic
1	teaspoon **each** dried basil leaves, dried oregano leaves **and** dried parsley flakes, crushed
1	teaspoon vinegar

1. Season the roast with the black pepper.

2. Put the potatoes, carrots, celery and tomato in a 3½-quart slow cooker. Top with the roast.

3. Stir the soup, water, garlic, basil, oregano, parsley flakes and vinegar in a medium bowl. Pour the soup mixture over the roast and vegetables.

4. Cover and cook on LOW for 10 to 12 hours** or until the meat is fork-tender.

5. Remove the roast from the cooker to a cutting board and let it stand for 10 minutes before slicing. Thinly slice the roast and put on a serving platter. Remove the vegetables with a slotted spoon and put on platter. Pour the juices from the cooker into a gravy boat and serve with the roast and vegetables.

For a thicker gravy, stir ½ **cup** water into ¼ **cup** all-purpose flour in a small bowl. Remove the roast from the cooker. Stir the flour mixture into the cooker. Turn the heat to HIGH. Cover and cook for 10 minutes or until the mixture boils and thickens.

*To roast the garlic, place a whole garlic bulb on a piece of aluminum foil. Drizzle with vegetable oil and wrap. Roast at 350°F. for 45 minutes or until soft. Peel and chop garlic.

**Or on HIGH for 5 to 6 hours

Asian Tomato Beef

Makes: 8 servings
Prep: 10 minutes
Cook: 7 to 8 hours 15 minutes

2   cans (10¾ ounces **each**) Campbell's® Condensed Tomato Soup (Regular **or** Healthy Request®)

⅓   cup soy sauce

⅓   cup vinegar

1½ teaspoons garlic powder

¼   teaspoon ground black pepper

3   to 3½ pounds boneless beef round steak, cut into strips

6   cups broccoli flowerets

Hot cooked rice

1. Stir the soup, soy sauce, vinegar, garlic powder, black pepper and beef in a 3½-quart slow cooker.

2. Cover and cook on LOW for 7 to 8 hours* or until the meat is fork-tender.

3. Stir the mixture. Add the broccoli. Turn the heat to HIGH. Cover and cook for 15 minutes or until the broccoli is tender-crisp. Serve over the rice.

Or on HIGH for 4 to 5 hours

Serving Suggestion Tip: Continue the Asian theme right through dessert. Slice and lightly toast pound cake. Top with canned Mandarin oranges in syrup and slivered almonds.

Slow Cooker Tuscan Beef Stew

Makes: 8 servings
Prep: 15 minutes
Cook: 8 to 9 hours 10 minutes

1 can (10¾ ounces) Campbell's® Condensed Tomato Soup (Regular **or** Healthy Request®)

1 can (10½ ounces) Campbell's® Condensed Beef Broth

½ cup Burgundy **or** other dry red wine **or** water

1 teaspoon dried Italian seasoning, crushed

½ teaspoon garlic powder

1 can (14½ ounces) diced Italian-style tomatoes

3 large carrots (about ¾ pound), cut into 1-inch pieces

2 pounds beef for stew, cut into 1-inch pieces

2 cans (about 15 ounces **each**) white kidney (cannellini) beans, rinsed and drained

1. Stir the soup, broth, wine, Italian seasoning, garlic powder, tomatoes, carrots and beef in a 3½-quart slow cooker.

2. Cover and cook on LOW for 8 to 9 hours* or until the meat and vegetables are fork-tender.

3. Stir in the beans. Turn the heat to HIGH. Cook for 10 minutes more.

Or on HIGH for 4 to 5 hours

Serving Suggestion Tip: Egg noodles are a lovely complement to this stew.